To

Best always —

REACHING THE
UNREACHABLE CHILD

REACHING THE
UNREACHABLE CHILD

Using Emotional Wisdom
To Help Children Recover
from Hopelessness and Negativity

Sheila Zaretsky, Ph.D.

Full Court Press
Englewood Cliffs, New Jersey

Published in the United States of America
by Full Court Press, 601 Palisade Avenue
Englewood Cliffs, NJ 07632

ISBN 978-0-578-03345-7

Library of Congress Control No. 2009933581

Editing and Book Design by Barry Sheinkopf for Bookshapers
(www.bookshapers.com)
Cover image courtesy istockphoto.com
Colophon by Liz Sedlack

To all those who have made my life worth living

preeminently my husband Sol and my delicious family,
Dr. Leslie Rosenthal (the most understanding guy in the world),
my students—who have taught me everything,
and my colleagues, who are always there.

Acknowledgements

My thanks go to Harriet Rosen, Veona Thomas, and Tippi Ullman, for their joyous support and hard-assed criticism; and to Dusty Sklar, for the praise and encouragement that was more than casual.

I also want to thank Barry Sheinkopf for his astute editorial counsel and tasteful book design.

TABLE OF CONTENTS

BEING THE CALM AND WISE ADULT
CHILDREN NEED IN ORDER TO THRIVE

WHAT MOTIVATES CHILDREN TO do well in school—and in life? Why is it that some are goal oriented and succeed while others hang back, turn away, or totally shut down? How can the unmotivated ones be reached? Finding answers to these questions became the focus of my twenty-five-year career in teaching, and it remains the focus of my second career as a psychotherapist.   This book tells what I have learned about the powerful inner forces that can lead to growth and success or to dysfunction and despair.   It is also about how to help children reverse their patterns of desolation and failure.

I found the answers when I began taking courses at an innovative psychotherapeutic program whose theories and techniques I was encouraged to apply in my inner city high school classroom.   It introduced me to a whole new universe of understanding and success with my students.

Children—the same as adults—are motivated by their emotions, which, to the extent that they have been traumatized, can become self-defeating. Their resultant behavioral difficulties accompany them in the classroom—and in the community, where adults have no choice but to address them.

In this book I will show how an adult's emotional understanding can reverse children's maladaptive dynamics. The therapeutic interchange I learned to practice as I went about my classroom routines enabled my difficult students (usually a handful at any given moment, but it might have been any of them at one time or another) to recover from their difficult moments and halt their downward spirals. In time, as our relationship deepened, they began to make the better decisions upon which their futures depended.

What worked, I found, is to replace the use of intimidation and condemnation with the communication of empathy, knowledge, and strength. Destructive behavior is always a child's way of coping with conflicted and anguished feelings, things they have no other way to conceptualize or endure. When they are responded to with informed compassion instead of the rejection they expect and therefore provoke, something shifts inside, rekindling a yearning to connect. The benevolent response of the knowledgeable adult reorients the child, encouraging them to cooperate and grow instead of repeating their old defiant or shut-down patterns.

While most teachers are aware of their students' need for understanding care and nurturance, the how-to of working with emotionally conflicted behavior is rarely addressed in literature on classroom management. The prevailing approaches too often neglect the children's inner sense of self: their painful memories and expectations, their conflicted loyalties, their hidden anxieties, their guilt, and their anger. Unaware of why, or even what, they have been feeling, at-risk children use the action patterns modeled for them at home or in their neighborhood. Without help, they have no way to think or talk about the frightening yet intangible forces in their minds that prevent them from cooperating. They need an adult who has learned the basics of healthy emotional response to help them manage and reorient themselves in more constructive ways.

In part, my helping children (and students of any age) is a way of helping the child in me. For example, I became able to understand and forgive myself for having been only an average student despite having high aptitude test scores. I discovered I was a lackluster student, not because of inability, but because of feelings that warned me above all to hide from those in authority. My psychotherapeutic training taught me that my anguish in school had not stemmed from my being "ridiculously shy and sensitive," the dismissive accusation I most often heard at home as well as from many teachers. In order to come out of hiding, what I needed was, not belittling descriptions of myself, but tolerance and guidance.

Learning this augmented my empathy for my students. Whether children in the inner city or graduate students in suburban New Jersey, all do their best when they have the opportunity to open up and explore the richness and turmoil of their inner lives. Their reluctance to expose themselves in the process of communication, the essence of classroom learning, melts away as I demonstrate my commitment to running my classroom as an emotional safe haven.

Mastering how to teach has been the odyssey of my adulthood, a voyage of discovery about the world of thinking, feeling, and motivation. An odyssey is a journey that eventually brings us home: when I teach others I continue to teach myself. Home for me is the mind and the emotional basis of our motivation. I want to teach what I have learned about trauma, survival, recovery, and resilience. Applying my therapeutic training in the classroom is the key that unlocked the emotional prisons of my students, and it also is what freed me from my own.

INTRODUCTION

WITNESS TO THE UNFOLDING OF TRAGEDIES

MY FIRST TEACHING JOB was in a junior high school located in an impoverished area of lower Manhattan. Twenty-three years old, raised in a middle-class suburban milieu, I was blindsided by what I faced in my classroom. Many of the children in my groups of thirty-five thirteen- and fourteen-year-olds were bent on defeating me! Yet it was a toss up whom I was more afraid of—my students or my supervisor, who with her killer stare could freeze an auditorium of wriggling young teens into sudden silence. I, too, felt terror in her presence. "You are a disaster, and I do not have the time to teach you," she snarled at me one day. Fortunately, she had me fired at the end of the year.

My next position was at a large, nearby high school where my department chairman, a gentle, six-foot-seven giant, patiently taught me the ABCs of teaching. "The most important part of a lesson is the motivation. Start off the first five minutes of class by capturing your students' interest. You might ask a question that connects the lesson to their lives," he continued, offering me several examples. Marveling at his gentleness, I realized that this was someone who would never bruise my spirit or threaten my students or me. His emphasis was on inspiring, not on intimidating, and I wanted to follow his lead.

What would attract my students' interest? What would arouse them to do their best? In the following years, as I deepened my interest in motivating even my most recalcitrant students, I realized that what I was dealing with extended beyond my classroom. When children were self-defeating with me, it reflected what went on in their lives outside of school and foretold how they would function as adults. I was a witness to the unfolding of tragedies.

Yet trying to coax performance out of the most unmotivated ones, usually about six to eight out of any group of thirty-five, was often a losing battle. Without their will harnessed to learning and growing, they would become dead weight, dragging themselves, their classmates, and me down. It made me realize how crucial it was to help them reverse their negativity, but how? Like Sheherazade I sought material enchanting enough to hold their interest, but still some would fall by the wayside. I felt as though I was carrying water in a sieve. Subsequently I learned that their truancy and failure patterns hold true for about thirty per cent of students in every social and economic class in this country. Thirty per cent of American children never graduate from high school, and in the inner city, that percentage is often doubled.

I also had a concern, which was, to paraphrase Galen's addendum to the Hippocratic oath, "First do no harm": I did not want to add further damage to whatever was inspiring my students' self-destructive choices. I had already discovered how impotent the traditional disciplinary tools were. Using them, i.e., scolding, giving bad grades, making phone calls home, or referrals to guidance counselors, wound up with the children vanishing into truancy or sliding into failure the same as ever. Having often striven to initiate what I thought was some rapport, I would feel stung as well as defeated. Though the administration of the school was aware of the problem, no one seemed to know how to reach that thirty per cent, not even truant officers.

Still I sought answers, taking workshops and reading whatever books and articles I could find in my attempt to understand the mindset of their behavior. And then as I was bemoaning my frustration with a colleague at the time clock one afternoon, I got the suggestion that changed my life. "You've got to check out this innovative program in applied psychotherapy!" she exclaimed, and gave me the details. Since I had benefited from engaging in my own personal psychotherapy, I thought, Interesting! It can't hurt to try.

In the very first course at the therapeutic program, I began to get the answers I had been seeking. The study of motivation is in fact the entire focus of psychotherapy. I learned that there is only one genetically endowed motivation to live a constructive life, and that it starts in infancy: the desire to please Mother. Over time, this desire transfers to Mother's symbols and substitutes, meaning other family members, teachers, and later bosses, leaders, intimates, and community. It also internalizes, becoming a desire to please the self. Yet I also learned that, given the wrong kind of response, the desire to please can invert to its opposite—the desire to oppose, to offend, or to escape. Thus, I learned that my truancy and failure-prone students were predisposed to failure before they ever met me.

In the classroom I symbolized the all-important mother of early childhood. Therefore, to help my resistant students get back on track, I had to get them to want to please me. The essence of how, I learned, was to build a nurturing relationship by giving them consistent doses of interest and understanding. This creates an emotional environment similar to the one a mother creates for a beloved child. In this way I was able to establish some trust, and then when students began to falter I could consult them about what was getting in the way of their sticking to their goals. Once they told me what was bothering them with their words, they stopped "telling" me with their defiant or oppositional behavior. The answers my students gave were often filled with conflict, pain, and anger. Getting to know them intimately, I could respond with compassion rather than admonishments. Over time this resulted in their wanting to attach to me and lean on me. Ultimately they became eager to be more like me, that is, able to live a constructive life.

Administering doses of informed understanding was easily done as I went about my daily classroom routines. And because it is based on the biology of the mind rather than on what feels right (i.e., to punish—punishing is always what feels right!), it has a powerful, enduring effect. An added plus, l was delighted to discover, is that understanding took none of the angst and energy that coercive or negative discipline had. Actually, classroom management became creative and fascinating. I learned that behavior always has unseen meanings, and that everyone makes complete sense once his or her story is known.

Children's conduct in school, from the best to the worst, conveys an inner world they have no way to conceptualize or put into words. The sunny ones, full of liking for themselves and others, unwittingly communicate that all is right inside them. No unbearable tensions disrupt their ability to be present and attentive. Anticipating that good things will happen, they are not burdened with dread or anger or conflict. When something does go wrong, they have the optimism to bounce back and recover.

But the edgy ones, the ones given to furtive ways of stealing attention, the ones compelled to defy rules or shut down sooner than give something of themselves to the teacher, are riddled with distrust, resentment, pessimism, and self-hatred. They draw negative responses as powerfully as a magnet attracts iron filings, suffer the consequences, and feel all the worse. But they have no idea of how—or why—they contribute to this state of affairs.

It has become my goal to help parents, teachers, and counselors learn how to recognize and address the way a child's behavior communicates his inner world. It is not something the child can do on their own. Only if they feel understood can they muster the strength and hope to face down their inner demons, and only then is their biological desire to connect with and please the adult rekindled. And there is another benefit to working in this therapeutic way—helping children talk about their feelings expands their emotional intelligence, their ability to reflect on and manage the hidden urges that cause their relationships to prosper or fail. Their potential to create a constructive future for themselves depends on their developing this ability.

I now use the same tactics with my graduate students as the ones I once used with my troubled inner city teens. I also use them with my family members, the greengrocer, the bus driver, and my surly neighbor over my back fence. I am ever more aware that no one is free of old, buried, tensions and conflicts stored in their complex brain. Knowing this helps me communicate empathetically and effectively, and not just with others, but also with myself.

CHAPTER 1

PREVENTING
ACADEMIC
SUICIDE

A. RECOGNIZING AND REVERSING A CHILD'S
HOPELESSNESS AND NEGATIVITY

MUCH OF MY ADULTHOOD has been dedicated to educating my younger self, a frightened child who devoted more energy to hiding from than to discovering the world. I want to help my younger self, and other people's younger selves, by bringing the hidden dynamics of our minds out of the dark shadows of lonely, painful obsession. I would like to help us all learn tolerance for the tendencies and patterns in ourselves that may have alarmed or repulsed us, for this is what frees us to grow and prosper. Compassionate self-knowledge enables us to become the person we want to be as well as to empathize with and help others.

Learning to use psychotherapeutic theories and techniques in my classroom, I discovered that the motivational core of the mind is the small and helpless child we once were. Just as back then, our feelings emerge from our appetites, our fears, our wishes to please our parents, and our desires to punish those who menace or thwart us. We also adopt aspects of our culture that may or may not be beneficial. But the most influential by far is our relationship with our mother. Because of my painful history with my own mother, agonizing recollections later skulked in my brain, hyper-alert to signal danger, when often there was none. From her responses to me over the years of my childhood, I had drawn the conclusion that I was woefully inadequate. We become ourselves in the mirror of our mothers' eyes.

I achieved independence at the age of twenty-one by moving to New York City directly upon graduating from college. I at once got an office job working for a clothing catalog where I handled footwear for the entire family. However, at the end of that year I learned that, to advance myself in the company, I would have to transfer to ladies' coats, a category for which I simply had no interest—so I made inquiries about how to become a teacher. Within a month of getting my first teaching position, I could not deny that, when my students performed poorly, they were not "stupid" or "bad." Rather, they were sabotaging both themselves and me. They all knew the importance of getting an education, but something inside them stopped them from adhering to this goal. The chips I could see on some of their shoulders on the first day of school, their balkiness in completing my assignments, and their truancy made no sense to me until I learned the importance of their emotions and their influences outside of school.

B. The power of understanding

The first class I took at the psychotherapeutic institute was called "Group Dynamics." Most of my classmates there were seasoned mental health professionals who discussed the therapy groups they were conducting. I, however, presented an eleventh-grade English class that met just before noon. The same lesson plan that I had used successfully with an equivalent group earlier in the day had fallen flatter than a lead balloon with this later group. Many of the students had sat slumped in their seats with their heads on their arms. Their main communications to me had been complaints about how boring my lessons were, pleas to use the bathroom pass, and requests as to know how many more minutes were left until the period would end. When I happened to mention to my Group Dynamics instructor the fact that most of them had not eaten breakfast, he'd interrupted me to exclaim, "They're starving! They can't learn on an empty stomach! You've got to feed them!"

At first I doubted this, telling myself, *Is he kidding?* But then I realized it was true—the kids were starving. So despite the school rule against eating in the classroom, I brought in sesame seed candies, graham crackers, and apples, saying, "I think I've been abusing you by expecting you to work on an empty stomach." Almost instantly the class came to life! Suddenly my lessons were interesting, challenging, and fun! One girl chirped merrily as she entered my room, "Where's our bird seed?" From this experience I learned that psychological "understanding" could take many forms.

Working with my students from the basis of understanding them, rather than trying to convince them to meet my expectations, was like a miracle. I discovered that, to reach the reluctant ones, I had to find out and address what they were communicating with their behavior. While in this first instance what worked was my recognition of their extreme hunger, in other instances it was often hidden negative feelings such as hopelessness or revenge. As I continued taking other psychotherapeutic courses, the usefulness of what I was learning kept me inspired. I realized that, without this knowledge base, my ability to know and communicate with my students had been compromised.

Foremost, I never again resorted to criticizing, demeaning, or threatening them. Those approaches only created further distance between us. Second, I learned to listen to them with a "third" ear, inferring what might be motivating them to resist. Besides their words, I considered their body language and behavior. In psychotherapeutic terms, my goal was to resolve their resistances to achieving success in my class. I mainly achieved this goal through interviewing them: *Me:* "How come I didn't get any homework?" *Student:* "I lost it." *Me:* "Can it be found?" *Student:* "No." *Me:* "Should I be concerned about your getting a failing grade?" *Student:* "Can I do it over?"

To interview them successfully, I had to help them feel safe enough to open up and speak about what was on their minds. Often they would not know, and I would use a therapeutic technique of helping them explore their thoughts and feelings. In this process they would start to feel understood, and they would gradually become freer of whatever conflicts had interfered with their achieving success in the past.

I had other striking successes. I had been assigned a homeroom class of "double holdovers"—children who had already failed tenth grade twice. This was an undesirable job generally foisted off onto younger staff, and I felt a twinge of dread as I glanced at my students' faces on the first day of school. I began to take attendance and handle administrative details with each child, moving row by row from the front to the back of the room. After I spoke with the last boy in the first row and turned my attention to the child at the front of the second row, I spotted the previous boy starting to sneak out my back door. I knew I had only seconds to lure him back.

"Whoa," I said in a light, non-confrontational voice. "How am I driving you out of the room? Is it my hairstyle? Did I wear the wrong skirt?" The boy looked at me as if I were a Martian but slid back into his seat. My intervention succeeded! I had used a "joining" technique, meaning I joined, or agreed, with his point of view. His body language had conveyed, "Phooey! I don't want to be with you," and my question confirmed that I understood his message and was willing to take the blame. At the same time I was inviting him to verbalize his criticism of me, though he remained mum. Each day that week he repeated the same drama, and each day I gave a variation of my original response: "What is it today—the pimple on my chin? My breath? Is it so bad you can smell it from way back there?" His facial expression continued to convey that I was weird, yet each day he would slide back into his seat. And then one day he remained seated without further ado.

Not long thereafter, he muttered to me after class as sort of an aside, "You're crazy, but you're smart." What was he thinking? On yet another day he asked if he could transfer into one of my English classes, and somehow we accomplished this mission. He also got into a class with me each following semester until he graduated three years later.

What greater proof could there have been of the efficacy of what I was learning? This boy with his history of failure and truancy had remained in school because of my responses. Whereas in the past I would have been intimidated by his glum expression and disheveled appearance (and a bit relieved if he had just vanished), I learned that, beneath his surly demeanor, he was an anxious and needy child the same as all the others.

My response to this boy—"How am I driving you away?"—had been designed to do three things: first, to protect his ego by my taking full credit for his behavior; second, to demonstrate my understanding that I was interested in keeping him with me regardless; and third, to lighten the mood of our interchange. I knew that it was not I *per se*, but I as symbolic of whoever had hurt him in the past, that he was flee-ing. The mind works through such symbolic manifestations, all un-beknownst to the child.

My new knowledge offered protection for my own ego as well as for his. In school a child's defiance is often seen as "disrespect," im-plying that the child consciously intends to insult *this* teacher. In a sense this is true, but it is not the teacher they want to hurt, but rather someone from their past. This was especially evident when a child behaved rudely on the first day of a new term, as in this instance. But as I grew more experienced, I discovered it was always the case. Learning this eliminated my ever feeling injured again, for I never again saw myself as having been the cause of the child's disrespect. And how could I want to punish someone who I knew was motivated by past frustration and pain? In place of trying to control such students through power or shame, I was learning to draw them into a relation-ship with me, harnessing the energy of their biological need to connect with a concerned parent symbol.

The fun and closeness I had with that glowering boy and the rest of his double-holdover class (using similar interventions) that semester was an eye-opener for them as well as for me. They would stare in fascination as I interacted with whoever was "acting up." One girl commented, with something like awe in her voice, "I think you like us!" It was true! As I tamed them, they became mine and I became theirs. Even the most defiant among them began to relate to me in a more relaxed and cooperative way. Helping my students with their emotional worlds, I became certain beyond a shadow of a doubt that using the traditional educational controls of logical or emotional pres-sure only reinforced their patterns of withdrawal into failure. If they felt faulted rather than understood as the traumatized souls they were, they hunkered deeper into their old habits of defiance or flight. But when they felt understood and respected, they responded with mounting willingness to trust and connect. Our time together became stress free, a mutual vacation from the pressures outside our classroom.

In more recent years, I have come up with a biological conception of how my approach worked. For one thing, when I gave understanding to my students, it often came out as humor, and we would all giggle and fool around for a bit. Laughter and fun stimulate the brain to produce opiods, natural brain hormones akin to "feel good" drugs such as opium and cocaine—the addictive substances to which my at risk children were tragically drawn. The brain produces them in "feel-good situations" like tender moments, trusted companionship, and rambunctious fun. Our playful moments together were antidotes to the frustrations and stresses of their outside lives. Further, as we had repeated pleasurable experiences together, new brain connections about how things could be in relationship to a teacher and to one another were forged. I often heard from other teachers about how they had had breakthroughs with one student or another whom I had "tamed." I never claimed credit, but I knew the miracle had begun when I helped those students feel at ease with me. Feeling more relaxed with other teachers, more changes and growth would occur in their brains. This is the transformational miracle of psychotherapy.

c. ADAPTING TO THE CHILD

I left that wonderful old neighborhood high school when Principal Edward A. Reynolds (who had also studied at the psychotherapeutic program) invited me to teach at West Side High School (renamed Edward A. Reynolds High School after his untimely death in 2002). A small alternative program serving mainly Harlem and the South Bronx, its six hundred students had been thrown out of an average of 2.5 schools before landing there as a last resort. They were all double holdovers. Ranging in age from fourteen to twenty, different ages were mixed together in small classes. More than a handful of the girls had babies, and the school had set up a day care program for them.

One of my first assignments was to teach Remedial Writing Skills. Oh, no! I thought. I can't make this work. Students will feel insulted by the very title of the class! But after the negative part of my mind had its say, I got an inspiration. (I have since discovered that saying, "No, I can't do it!" to myself often brings an "Oh, yes I can!" in the backwash, along with an idea about how to solve whatever problem.) What if I made the class into an imaginary business? Each student could be an "employee," and we could have "staff meetings" in place of class sessions. The writing/learning tasks could come out of this context. I wanted it to be a business that would provide a range of gratifying "jobs." The idea of a resort hotel popped into my mind, given that it would communicate to the students my understanding of their emotional needs. Remedial students generally feel hopeless and pessimistic about success, so that learning seems a tedious exercise leading nowhere. My imaginary business would address their need for fantasy and pleasure with a gradual exposure to the frustrations of working on their writing skills. Playing out this fantasy would be fun for me, too.

I had in mind Bruno Bettelheim's book *The Uses of Enchantment* (1977), in which he writes about adolescents' need for optimism about their future, which to them looks grim and undoable. He talks about how traditional fairy tales and folk stories portray a character of humble origin who, by overcoming obstacles through his own resourcefulness, serves as a model for the child reader. Bettelheim believes that years of fantasies of this sort (as well as a belief in magic) are needed for children to develop a positive view of adulthood. Children must have enough hope to overcome their feelings of inadequacy, dependency, impatience, and sibling rivalry. Optimism is essential to develop their rationality in the face of their internal gloom.

When my remedial writing class convened for its first meeting, I told them the plan and gave them their initial assignment: to think of a name for our new corporation. After some discussion they chose *Fantasy Inn*. I realized they had in mind a television program of that time called *Fantasy Island*, a resort where guests could achieve their deepest wishes with the help of a host with magical powers. Something magical began to happen in my classroom: instead of the atmosphere of sullen resistance I had anticipated, there was an almost giddy feeling of excitement. We discussed the many employees we would need: social directors, managers, security staff, sports professionals, entertainers, waitresses, bartenders, croupiers, and chefs. Each member of the class chose a job.

Their first assignment, which was to write resumes applying for these jobs, brought on instant dismay. It was as if I had asked them to write something in a language they did not know. I knew they needed my help, and I accepted this about them, so together we constructed their resumes, line by line. When, for example, some of them complained that they had never had jobs and so could not put anything under *Job Experience,* I found out each had done work at home such as shopping, laundry, and childcare. I suggested the resume entry *Household Consumer Management*—a modern, businesslike phrase.

Another entry blank on their resumes was *Salary*. "What should we put?" they asked.

"What would be the right amount for an executive of a first-class business?," I replied. Several answered five to ten thousand dollars a year. Others, worldlier yet still childlike in their thinking, suggested fifty thousand, but then where on earth would I—teacher—get such a sum? Looking around our dingy classroom, a few wanted to know where their "offices" would fit. It was clear that some of them could not at first grasp the notion that we were engaging in a fantasy. For all their mature physical presence, they were still locked into the concrete thinking of a small child.

Some students made sadistic and depressed comments about themselves or their classmates such as, "I ain't never gonna get no first- class job." Since they tended to react to insults and slights with physical violence or withdrawal, I wanted to model for them a different response, viz, how to shrug off negative comments, so I gave them a rule that they were not allowed to criticize themselves or each other, only me. As a result there was almost no "mean" talk in my room, and what little there was I could always head off at the pass. Two girls, for example, frequently sucked their thumbs, their other fingers curled against their noses as a toddler would do. When members of the class started to ridicule them for this behavior, I broke in: "What's wrong with it? It helps them to relax in this stressful world. And there are no side effects!"

"Staff meetings" warmed up as class members began to feel at home and to realize that I really meant it when I told them, "We can talk about anything when we brainstorm in our business meetings here. We've got to help one another find solutions to our challenging business problems." As an English teacher as well as a psychotherapist, I knew that talking comes before writing. I also knew that my alternative school remedial students especially needed a lot of talk in order to feel at home with a new subject, as well as to relieve their hidden, inner tensions.

They tested me by digressing from a topic at hand to allude to acts of defiance or drug use. They might refer provocatively to sex or complain about feeling tired and hungry. Wanda, a tall, pretty girl with memorably dark, curly eyelashes, piped up out of the blue to ask, "Who here likes oral sex?" It brought on hoots and jeering, but Wanda really wanted to talk about oral sex.

Michelle, a bright but cynical girl, broke in: "Yeah, I wish some guy would eat me out, and then I would never let him forget it. I would tell the whole world what he had done." Her tone of voice was leaden with anger. I wondered who had hurt her and what she was revealing about her life. I felt a mixture of feelings—a bit shocked, but also empathetic, and I realized their sadism and tendency to ridicule and spite one another did not come out of thin air.

In my classes at the psychotherapeutic program I was learning that talking, even in the guise of "fooling around," was the best way to recover from trauma. After a frightening experience such as a visit to the dentist, a child comes home and plays dentist on his toys, his pets, his siblings, and anything else available, until he gets it out of his system. My students were working on their frightening and frustrating lives. Though they often squealed as if they were having fun, undertones of anxiety were evident. Their experiences with the opposite sex had often been far from friendly. They knew the risks of their impulsive behavior— AIDS was making headlines at that time, plus there was always the potential for other sexually transmitted diseases, not to mention the violence that can erupt from jealousy, passion, and betrayal. They had seen these things in their families and neighborhoods. They were aware that sex was a way of playing with fire.

I knew not to lecture them, for it only causes selective deafness. Instead I thought about their words. If I felt alarm, I might ask in a mild voice, "Should I be concerned that something will happen and I won't get to see you any more?" My questions always focused on protecting the ongoing relationship with me, for that was the key to my having an influence over them. In effect, I often loaned them my anxiety. Also, I often laughed with them instead of expressing "proper" disapproval of their tomfoolery or use of "forbidden" language. The overriding necessity was to get them talking, opening up, and feeling at home with me. Yes, they were challenging me by saying certain words; all had had experiences in other classrooms of being punished for such usage. But my aim was to narrow the gap between us, and I knew how essential it was for them to stray off topic into talking about their lives. Even though these children were teenagers, they still had a lot of growing up to do. They needed to have safe, constructive fun sanctioned by an interested, nonjudgmental adult.

To expect children to act more mature than they are capable of is unrealistic and only adds to their self-hatred and despair. I had the idea that our mixture of play and work exemplified a positive family experience in which children are gradually prepared for the challenges of adult life. I relied on my feelings to know when to pull them out of a digression. "Okay, staff, back to work. I need your answers to this problem we are facing."

I mined the business fantasy for themes for writing projects. My students wrote descriptions of how they wanted their offices to look. I provided architectural magazines for them to get ideas about furniture, carpets, and window treatments, and they put a lot of interest into their selections. Later, they wrote business letters corresponding with the suppliers for their respective departments, requiring that they state clearly and directly what they needed. Subsequently, to expose them to the disappointments of reality in the safety of our fantasy regime, I told them that their supplies had come in damaged, so they had to write letters to their suppliers asking to be compensated. Despite their initial impulses to retaliate, they wrote clear explanations of what was wrong and what they wanted done in recompense.

They also wrote replies to the complaints of customers. Everyone got a cranky letter from a certain customer who had a criticism about each of their departments: her room was dirty and had a bad smell, her food was not hot enough, the tennis balls did not bounce, she did not meet any interesting men, and so forth. Our business meeting on this topic got rowdy: "Screw her. She can go shove it. We don't need her business," one student smirked. But then I told them what an excellent customer she was, visiting us at least once every season. Also she referred other customers to us, plus she never asked for a discount. Their eventual letters to this customer quite surprised me. They were actually charming, and in each case offered a special premium to make amends.

They wrote culinary reviews for the chef, after first protesting that they had never eaten in a downtown restaurant, and what was that nasty stuff called "caviar" anyway? They wrote entertainment reviews for the social director to help him select new talent. They also wrote letters to the chairman of the board (me), giving their recommendations about various problems that arose, some of which I extracted from their spontaneous talk. For example, several students drew attacks from the others by identifying themselves through their dress and talk as homosexual, so I gave the class the task of deciding whether to entertain a homosexual group for a certain weekend, or a retired teachers' group who wanted a deep discount, or a paraplegic group who would need extra help with their disabilities. They immediately ruled out the paraplegic group, saying, "We don't want to wipe the shit off anybody's butts." Then they had fun criticizing the "cheap-o" teachers, and one boy kept slyly repeating, "No faggots in this hotel!" But finally, after considerable discussion and to my surprise, one student spoke up to say that it would not be fair to discriminate against a group because of its sexual orientation. Everyone agreed, and they all wrote recommendations to me accordingly!

Since I was aware of their drug experimentation and use, I had them write about what they planned to do about personnel in each of their departments who had addiction problems. As usual, the discussion began with some wild remarks. One boy said he knew a drug dealer who made as much in one week as I made in a whole year. "Does he have health insurance and a pension plan?" I asked. But in their essays on this topic they took the welfare of their employees seriously, suggesting rehab and medical treatment.

On one occasion, a student fed me a new theme by asking, "What is going to happen in this business next? Now, don't tell me there's going to be a murder in this hotel!" Taking the hint, I cooked up a situation in which they had all witnessed a homicide. Their job was to write a description of the perpetrator and the deed for the police inspector. Several identified the perpetrator as me and the victim as a child. I had the idea that they were giving themselves the pleasure of defaming and triumphing over me, which I again understood as their working on hurts and betrayals from other adults in their past. The murder scenes couldn't have been more gruesomely detailed: body parts were chopped off and flung dripping against the walls, etc. I laughed as merrily as they at these depictions.

Anticipating the end of the school year, I posed a question relevant to our coming separation. The corporation that owned our business wanted to automate much of the work that they had been doing. Their writing task was to convince the chairman of the board (me again) to continue employing them instead of saving money by replacing them with robots. A very sad assignment, but saying good-bye at the end of June was a very sad time. Their responses showed that they all knew I would never trade them in for machines.

The teaching assignment that I had dreaded became a delight. Why? From the outset I refused to act the role of the schoolmarm relentlessly red-penciling her way through her students' souls. The children in that alternative school, riddled as they were with hopelessness and unmet needs from their early lives, didn't need me to add to their toxic burden. Their thumb sucking, their constant eating, their greedily helping themselves to the supplies I provided, their poor work habits, their tendency to engage in bullying and spiteful behavior, their magical thinking, all indicated their need to do the fantasy work that leads to optimism and the strength to face the future.

The "magic potion" I offered was the acceptance of this need and the environment in which to work on it. In the "staff discussions" of our fantasy business, kept afloat by pride in their executive status, my students flooded me with their chaotic thoughts and feelings. They helped me and one another sort them out in the guise of freewheeling, often playful discussion. Our work together provided an antidote to the traumatic aspects of their lives, adding some hope, pleasure, and courage to hearten them for what lay ahead. With each business problem, the class could hardly wait to hear what their classmates had written. By the year's end, their "personnel file folders" bulged with writing samples that were fresh and meaningful, yet as edited as any writing examination could demand.

D. ANTICIPATING IMMATURITY AND IMPULSIVITY

Every uncooperative or anti-social act, from coming late to class, to getting poor grades, to preying on other children, to drug use, to truancy, is a child's way of communicating underlying frustration and despair. It is not done consciously. Ask a child why they have committed a destructive act, and they will usually say, "I don't know," or speak about wanting to retaliate for some recent frustration. They may even think of it as a way to have fun, but if so it is in the vein of spiteful retaliation. Underneath, they dimly realize that such pleasure is short-lived and leads only to further negative exchanges and painful isolation. On some level, children realize that change can only come from adult intervention, yet their way of trying to get what they need is by showing and provoking rather than speaking.

Children in despair believe that sacrificing themselves, such as by endangering or hurting themselves, is the only way to get adults to wake up and pay attention. Until they are helped to put words to their internal chaos, they tend to conceal their smoldering hurt, disappointment, and anger. On some level they want to protect the adults on whom they depend from their anger and need. If help is still not forthcoming, they blame themselves all the more, fantasizing, *If I ruin myself, then they'll really feel sorry and treat me better.* They usually have seen others in their family exhibit such behavior as well. Academic suicide—failure in school—is an unhappy child's favorite way of getting back at their parents. It is at once a cry for help, an act of revenge, and a self-punishment.

In truth, every child needs some help controlling his unruly impulses. (I could say the same of most human beings of any age.) Sitting passively for many hours a day in a classroom is not the behavior our evolution designed for our hunter-gatherer or agrarian ancestors. However, evolution did design children to want to please the important adults in their lives. Schoolchildren need empathy in this quandary. They also need understanding for the fact that their natural impulse is to learn through active play. Often it is when teachers introduce some fun or a game or fantasy into their classroom activities that students come to life. Playfulness is children's way of researching what the world is about, and it is the ambience in which they feel most at home.

I doubt that inflicting punishment and condemnation on a hurting or angry child is ever constructive. Yes, a child must be restrained from hurting others or damaging others' property. At the very least, a time out for cooling off may be needed. Having the child sit next to the teacher for ten or fifteen minutes is one way to do this. If the child has destroyed property, reparation is important. The child might do community service—washing chalkboards or the like. Making amends helps the child feel worthy again.

Not long ago I read an article about a dyslexic child who had handed in a competently written essay with the help of his older brother. But his teacher had responded, "This is not your work! I'm going to tear it up and give you a failing grade!" Had she taken a few moments to cool down, the teacher would probably have acknowledged that hers was not a helpful response, however great her outrage. (We must keep in mind that feelings are from the reptilian brain, not from the intelligent neocortex.) It is also likely that the teacher's reaction stemmed from memories of instances when she had suffered herself as a child.

From my viewpoint, a better response to the dyslexic child would have been first to praise his work, affirming his impulse to please the teacher, however misguided it seemed on first impression. Next the teacher could explore how the child's remarkable improvement had come about. When he is consulted rather than challenged, the child will acknowledge the truth. The teacher can then decide how to proceed. She might welcome the brother's help as a resource for the child, perhaps capitalizing on it in the future. If she wanted a different behavior from the child, she might guide him in that direction. "For the future, this is what I would like you to do. . . ." The past can never be fixed; only the future can. Most importantly, this consultative approach will not traumatize the child and damage the teacher/child bond.

Professionals are human, too. Before giving up familiar ways of controlling children, teachers need the courage of their convictions and the leadership and support of their supervisors. Their own early school experiences may have created difficult memories that linger as disturbing and mostly unconscious pressures. Teachers, too, may need the opportunity to learn and practice new ways of thinking before changing their approach. But if their supervisors model an emotionally intelligent response, teachers will be far more likely to be willing to do the same.

Somehow, compelling new information from neuroscience and psychodynamic psychology needs to be brought into the culture of the school. A child's brain is not the same as an adult's. The prefrontal cortex, the part of the brain that exercises good judgment, self-control, consideration for others, cooperation, and gratification delay, does not start to function consistently and well until around the age of twenty-five (women) to thirty (men). Logic, threat, and shame cannot work if children do not yet have the mental structures to control themselves consistently and well. Instead, what punishment teaches is revenge, counter-revenge, hatred, and self-hatred.

A better approach is to anticipate the reality of children's immaturity. Adults can then lend their own ego strength and skill until such time as the child matures and incorporates the adults' model. Prevention should be the first step. Just as parents learn to baby-proof their house, teachers could keep temptations out of reach. Doing so could range from teachers keeping their valuables under lock and key, to anticipating how overwhelmed many students will be by certain assignments and therefore giving them whatever help they need, to interceding before children get over-stimulated and lose control as they typically do around holidays or special events. Secondly, instead of expecting children to be able to cooperate unfailingly, teachers could conceive of part of their role as helping children do the right thing. This would entail anticipating which children will need extra vigilance. (In other words, keeping in mind that a bit more patience and skill will be necessary for a few.) Also, sometimes children with more maturity are able to help those who are less able to stay in control. Third, when a child does engage in an undesirable behavior, instead of condemning them, the teacher could conceive of their task as helping them enact more desirable behavior in the future.

Not long ago I read a newspaper article about how an entire town's board of education went into an uproar when it found that children were plagiarizing material after having learned to do research on the internet. How much more constructive it would have been if the teachers had anticipated that children would look for an easy solution to a task that seemed new and formidable to them. They could then have helped children not be seduced by this temptation by consulting them: "What if anything is going to make doing this project difficult for you? Should I be concerned that access to research material on the internet will tempt you to plagiarize?" Many children will never even have heard the word "plagiarize," and will have no idea that it is a prosecutable crime! "Have I given you enough support so that you can do it without using the illegal, easy way? Is there any further help you would like from me?"

My emphasis is on how difficult and complex it is to be human, let alone a child. I acknowledge that it feels far more natural and satisfying to punish than to give children understanding. Geneticists consider punitive revenge a natural trait of all animal species. But to advance civilization, we need solutions that are based on long-range goals rather than short-term satisfactions. Helping young people to be motivated to obey the rules because of their relationship with us is what will facilitate their becoming problem solvers rather than problem-creators in the long run.

E. Enforcing Rules Without Negativity

Students at any age level learn best when they feel emotionally secure. From earliest infancy, a major task of the educator is to guard the child from overly stressful stimuli. When the teacher (as symbolic parent) insulates the child from trauma in the classroom, the child develops trust and views the created world as a place where they can grow and learn. Eventually the child internalizes their experience, adding a valuable input to their sense of inner security and self-confidence. If their later teachers reinforce this, the outcome will be a child with resilience and confidence in difficult circumstances. Moreover, instead of using their energy to exhaust and defeat the teacher, the child will join in the cooperative classroom endeavor.

It is the learner's first school, their family, that sets the template for later learning experiences. When early nurturing goes well enough, the child connects challenges such as learning something new with feelings of excitement and satisfaction. A small child is a mad scientist, eager to explore every centimeter of their environment. When accidents and frustrations born of their explorations are understood as normal and expectable, their spirited curiosity is kept alive.

Anxiety can actually shut down the cognitive functioning of a child's brain, as neuroscientists have observed in the laboratory study of animals. For example, when a young rat is subjected to trauma, it cannot learn a simple task that its nontraumatized littermates accomplish with ease. Similarly, a human subject who has been made anxious has a much more difficult time solving a problem than someone who is unruffled. Those with posttraumatic stress syndrome may be unable to attend to learning at all.

Teachers do not have much influence on what goes on in a child's home, but by making their classrooms into emotional sanctuaries, they can provide a restorative environment. The basics of teaching in an emotionally protective way are simple to describe: Use no negative reinforcers such as harsh or sarcastic tones of voice or rejecting body gestures. (Such negative responses exacerbate what alienated the child from relating cooperatively in the first place.) Instead, conceive of the teacher's task as assisting children to follow rules and instructions.

F. THE CONSTRUCTIVE USE OF CONSEQUENCES

Consequences, not punishments, socialize children in a positive way. A failing grade is a consequence, not a punishment. I might ask a child, "Hmm—it looks like I cannot pass you this marking period," inviting a discussion. It may turn out that the child has a personal reason for failing; alternately, they may have had the idea they could get away with murder by exercising their charm, sneaking under the wire, or exhausting me. They are not "bad" for trying such ploys—which after all are solutions they have learned in the past—but they need to learn additional ones if their goal is to do well.

Rules and consequences are most effective if they are discussed and agreed upon in advance. Children appreciate the opportunity to talk about what is expected of them, and the opportunity to protest—not necessarily to overrule, but to express their complaints. As I have observed innumerable times, they often need to say "no" before they can say "yes." Failing is sometimes just a way of saying the important word "no" in a relatively safe environment.

The word "no" comes before "yes" in a child's development. Just before the age of two, as the child begins to talk, they discover their power to influence their environment. This is an essential foundation for their mental health. Observe how eighteen-month-old to two-year-old toddlers are in love with the word "no!" I can remember one toddler at the peak of his "terrible twos" saying, "No!" to the offer of an ice-cream cone. His eyes said, "Yes!" but his verbal answer was emphatically "No!" Many people can observe the residue of their two-year-old selves in their own impulses to say, "No, I don't want to," or, "No, I can't!" as their first responses to a request. Once having said it, at least to themselves, they may be surprised to find they want—or at least are willing—to do whatever it is after all. For this reason students saying "no" needn't dismay a teacher, whether they say it with their words or with their behavior. If the teacher gently persists in a non-critical way, "no" will convert to "yes" as children realize they do not really want the consequence of a failing grade.

At around the age of three, children learn to say, "Yes," signifying their emotional readiness to cooperate. But if there was significant trauma in their earlier years, they may have trouble getting to the "yes" stage. Not until they have had the opportunity to get their fill of the feeling of power that can only be gotten by using the word "no" can they give up having to defy the authorities in their environment.

Rules and consequences are best given in a neutral, matter-of-fact manner, so that negativity is not aroused. The idea is to help children become aware that they are actually making a choice when they break a rule or defy an order (assignments are orders). Mistakes, on the other hand, should be understood as just something that all humans do. It is essential to convey the idea that the teacher is available if the child needs assistance in following rules or directions. Plus, the teacher has to be prepared to meet some immaturity, unpreparedness, and negativity in any group. Children do not really understand why they behave in a regressed or defiant way. They are often not even fully aware as they do it. A child cannot have the perspective on himself that a teacher can.

g. FACING UNRULINESS FEARLESSLY

Using my approach in an unruly classroom, I begin by becoming very still but at the same time showing no dismay, anger, or impatience. It has been my experience that, within a minute or two, the students will begin to fall silent. This has proven true of even the most disorderly groups of excited adolescents I have ever encountered. At some point they realize they cannot get me to try to fight with them. I won't do it, yet I have all the power, and my quiet, attentive stance shows it. The burden of responsibility shifts to where it belongs—inside their psyches. They start shushing and poking one another with their elbows. "Look at the teacher," they whisper. As the group settles into attentive quiet, an atmosphere of anxiety arises. Children tune in to their need for their caregivers if the adult remains undistracted by their overstimulation.

A therapeutically trained guidance counselor told me about a nine-year-old girl who had been referred to her for acting up in class. The girl had only recently transferred to the guidance counselor's school after having been expelled from a former placement. Once the counselor established rapport with the child, she mildly asked what had led to the expulsion. "My teacher didn't like me!" the girl replied. She went on to say that this was what had motivated her to be as bad as she could be at that old school! In her meetings with the guidance counselor, the child was always asking for things. She would look greedily around the office and plead, "Can I have this?" "Can I have that?"

To work with her in a way that addressed her unmet need for the love and attention that these items represented, the guidance counselor commiserated, "You know, sometimes I wish I could have all the goodies in the whole, wide world." Together the guidance counselor and the small girl fantasized about what that would be like, symbolically addressing the child's feelings of deprivation. After meeting regularly with the guidance counselor for some months, the girl became more tractable in her classroom.

Teachers who work with children from deprived backgrounds do well to address students' unmet needs by creating an atmosphere of abundance. Items like paper, pencils, crayons, tissues, and Band-Aids can be made available. Birthdays can be celebrated with treats. Writing lessons on the theme of, "If I won the lottery. . ." or "If I owned a toy store. . ." are also effective. I have observed such children take great handfuls of supplies, or of sweets on the occasion of a celebration, and I always encourage them, "Help yourself! There are lots more in the closet." Though a teacher can never totally make up for what a child has lacked, these symbolic gestures work bit by bit to neutralize past disappointments and frustrations.

Children's presenting behavior, for all its disruptiveness, embodies the way they learned to endure in their lives. They may have found that being chaotic lent them some shelter from the unpredictable violent behavior of their parents or caregivers, and in this sense provided a survival strategy. (This is why helping students feel safe with him or her enables a teacher to create a new beginning for them, laying down new memory patterns and stimulating new thoughts and brain cell growth.)

Agitation in a child most often communicates anxiety. Anthony was a dervish of motion as he entered my classroom for the first time. "Am I making you nervous?" I asked in a respectful voice.

I took responsibility for his behavior even as I began to educate him about his feelings. "Come sit," I said to him, twenty-five times a day for the first two months. "Come sit by me," and I helped him to relax.

Silliness is another communication of distress. Fifteen-year-old Shawn was shallow and impulsive when his parole officer first brought him to the alternative school where I taught. Shawn had begun acquiring a criminal record at the age of ten. In my class he obsessed about sexual organs. I used a behavioral technique of withholding any hint of annoyance as I studied him, and gradually he became more appropriate. After I had worked with him for a year, Shawn announced one day that he had had a dream about me. "I dreamed I was having sex with you," he said teasingly—but then amended, "No, I dreamed you were making food for me, and it was good." He was telling me in the symbols of his dream that my food—my teaching—was good. Education is food for thought, fed by the teacher. In time Shawn became known for his studiousness, and today is a high school teacher himself.

It is always true that children's unruly behavior has little or nothing to do with the current teacher. Fully expecting that they are about to get the same dreaded outcome as they got with their earlier care givers, children in effect engage in a preemptive strike. When a teacher employs emotionally informed techniques, however, the child has the opportunity to reverse their expectation. As they develop trust in the teacher, they establish a new feeling of comfort and ease when under another's authority. Later they transfer their new expectation onto relationships with other trustworthy authorities in their lives. This is the hidden process and outcome of psychotherapy.

When difficult children are not met with negative responses, they cannot help becoming intrigued, for deep down they still have that inborn desire to please their caregivers. Memories in their emotional brains may continue to predict that they will be misunderstood and even devastated, but eventually a new expectation can be securely established.

H. HAVING EMPATHY FOR THE INHERENT PAINFULNESS OF LEARNING

Students also need empathy because learning is inherently painful. In order to learn, we have first to be willing to feel ignorant and dumb. Until we learn a new discipline and master a body of knowledge, we are ignorant and dumb! Every teacher has encountered know-it-alls who cannot learn because they cannot tolerate feeling stupid. Further, because the brain both seeks and resists novelty, we have to contend with the normal part of students' minds that just doesn't want to be bothered with something new. This is especially so if new experiences in the past were painful. What is helpful is just to expect that some children will balk at learning. They may need to say "No, I can't!" or "No, I won't!" a few more times before they are ready to say "Yes!"

i. Working with the child's goals

I always establish a contract with my students, taking care to frame it with goals that are theirs, not mine. Do they want to pass? Do they want to distinguish themselves by getting a good grade? Or do they have something else in mind? This helps them realize that when they resist, they are resisting their own objectives, not mine. The children learn that they have the power to create either a desirable or an undesirable outcome for themselves. As long as the teacher remains neutral and does not invoke the child's defiance by using an accusatory tone of voice, the child will get the point. The power struggle between teacher and student ends, and the teacher's task shifts from pressuring the child to do something they are reluctant to do, to finding out what prevents them from fulfilling their own stated goal.

Observing a child who is not working, the teacher can ask: "What is stopping you from doing this assignment?" Notice that the spotlight in this question is on the word "what," and not on the word "you." Keeping the spotlight off of the child's weak ego insulates them from feeling assaulted by a superior power. As the teacher repeatedly interacts in this consultative way, he or she gradually trains the student to reflect and problem solve about their own inner process. He or she also helps them feel safe enough to ask for help, another enhancement for their emerging goal orientation. It does not take long for children to realize that when they try to defeat the teacher, they are actually defeating themselves. However, it is not helpful to lecture the child. Students are far more likely to follow through on the solutions that come out of their own mouths.

Some of the reasons why students resist doing an assignment may have to do with concrete issues in their lives—there may be excessive demands being placed on them at home; they may not have a quiet place to study; they may need additional help, or one-on-one tutoring. Another possibility is that the child may not understand what is being asked of them. The student from a chaotic home may lose or misplace materials and be too fearful to bring this to the teacher's attention. The child may be so filled with anxiety about a situation at home or in their neighborhood that they cannot think about anything else—excessive anxiety derails concentration. Some of these situations are readily solvable, and others may take time or even be intractable.

Except sometimes the teacher will get the feeling that a child is simply not interested in finding a way to do what needs to be done. It is likely that such a child will passive-aggressively defeat any attempt made to help them. In this case, it is best to back off. Know that, for such a child, it is more important to establish their autonomy than to advance in school at this given moment. Since such students get gratification from depriving the teacher of the pleasure of helping them (keeping in mind that it is not the teacher *per se*, but the teacher as symbolic other from their past, whom they wish to defeat), it is a waste of breath to try to force the issue. They are in a desperate struggle to gain the beachhead of self-rule that they had been unable to attain at the proper age of two. This must be respected.

By stepping back, the teacher affirms this hidden need, and most often this alone will bring about the desired result. In any event, not only do children have a right to fail in school, there is no way to force them to do otherwise. When teachers refrain from engaging in a power struggle around this issue, they also take away the satisfaction in defeating them. Deprived of this gratification, children have to find a new way to manage their impulses. It can even be helpful to acknowledge that the teacher has no objection to their failing, but if they should change their minds the teacher would welcome helping them do what they need to do in order to pass.

I once had a student who sat with his head on his desk day after day. He wasn't unruly in any other way than simply stonewalling me and refusing to do anything I asked. When I tried to contact him, he would just shrug and avert his face from mine. On parent/teacher night, his mother initiated our discussion by telling me that she was determined to make him keep his bathroom clean, but he was equally determined not to do so. "I will ground him until he is forty years old if I have to," she said, frightening me with her intensity. Suddenly I was able to understand her child.

Some parents disagree with the approach of letting their child develop their own readiness. They insist on finding a way to force them to do something they are currently refusing to do. Parents also benefit from the same management techniques as the children. Affirm their feelings: "Your job as a parent is the most difficult one there is, bar none. Children can be maddening! Plus, you get no thanks!" Consult them: What techniques have they tried so far? What in their opinion is the child saying with their behavior? Has anything worked in the past? How would they think it best to work with the child's negativity? What has their pediatrician suggested? Have they considered consulting the school's child guidance department? Have they considered attending a parenting workshop to get other answers? Are they aware that the use of force has been correlated with suicide?

The use of consequences need not lead to a power struggle. Here is the way attendance was handled when I was working at Edward A. Reynolds High School: If a child missed more than six days in a marking period, they would begin to lose credit fraction by fraction (excellent way to teach decimals and percentages). "Oh, my goodness," the teacher would note to a student approaching their fourth absence. "It looks like you are about to start losing some credit. Should I be concerned about this?" The consequence here is loss of credit, not a teacher out to inflict guilt.

Detached children often try to make it seem like the teacher is arbitrarily punishing them. The student might whine, "If you liked me you'd let me get by, just this once." One persuasive response to this ploy is, "Would a good teacher break the rules?" Some interesting ethical dialog might ensue: "Rules are made to be broken," I have heard some children say. "Hmmm. But then I might kill somebody!," I would observe, and we'd both laugh.

While it is essential to let consequences impel the child to do some thinking, at the same time it is useful to provide them with help in obeying the rules. I learned to give guidelines. For example I would declare, "I want you to come to school unless you have a fever of over 101 degrees." This often met with protests such as, "But I don't feel good! You want me to suffer?" I would respond, "If you have a cold, you will feel miserable whether you are at home or in school, so you might as well be in school with me where you are working toward your future and I get the pleasure of your company." Often inner city children would say, "I don't live for the future. I might be dead by then," revealing their fatalism. Then we can pull out a teacher's trump card, our knowledge of their hidden wish to please us: "Then come for me. I want you here with me, every day."

1. T<small>EACHING</small> M<small>ANNERS</small>

Some children would deliberately offend me. Let me illustrate with Katy. She and I had already formed a bond when the following scenario occurred. It was as if she assumed I would let her get away with murder, since she had learned I would respect her emotionally no matter what. All I knew about Katy's history was that she had grown up in a violent home. One day as I was trying to put a bundle of student papers into my briefcase, Katy approached me and said, "I need you to do something for me," whereupon she abruptly snatched my papers right out of my hands.

I was thunderstruck! Nonetheless, after exhaling to calm myself, I seized the opportunity to work on her functioning more appropriately. "Looks like you want me to hate you today!" I exclaimed. "What's going on?"

Crestfallen, Katy shoved my papers back at me. Moments later, she turned to me once more and asked, "Do you still hate me?"

"Only when you are hateful," I replied. My goal was to teach her but not to devastate her. In addition to demonstrating the importance of being respectful when she wanted something, I wanted her to learn that feelings like hate and being hated can be talked about without having to end a friendly bond.

Days later, Katy again interrupted me in an obnoxious way, on this occasion to request a letter of recommendation. "You sure don't know how to get what you want from me," I snapped.

"What do you mean?" Katy asked, again sounding astonished and hurt.

"You come in wanting me to do something for you and instead you give me the feeling of wanting to shoot you."

"But I need this," she whined.

"So why don't you give me the feeling of wanting to do it for you?" I persisted.

"Damn, I thought you was my godmother," Katy dodged.

"What does that have to do with anything?" I asked.

After a few seconds' pause, Katie said, "Okay. Please, my dear, sweet teacher. Would you write a job recommendation for me?" It turned out she did know how to be appropriate! In the warmth of our relationship she became willing to give up the hostile manner she had learned elsewhere. The miracle of my engaging in this psychothera-peutic way with her is that she became reliably well mannered there-after, not just with me but also with other teachers and students, and in time with her boss, her love interest, and so forth. She had inter-nalized my appropriateness. And that is how children learn.

CHAPTER 2

THE EMOTIONAL
FACTS OF LIFE

A. Befriending the Full Range
of Human Feelings

PRIDE/VANITY, ENVY, GLUTTONY, lust, anger, greed, and sloth: These were once called "the seven deadly sins." To me, however, they sound like an ordinary Sunday afternoon's moods and pastimes. Why were they once considered lethal? Simply having a feeling cannot actually hurt us or anyone else. It is putting a feeling into action, rather than the feeling itself, that can cause harm.

Feelings are some of the many mental processes constantly at work in our brain. We also have goals and knowledge and strategies constantly at play in our thoughts. It is our ability to think reflectively that integrates our mind and keeps us sanely in balance. The habit of reflection is achieved through the use of language—reading, talking, and sharing our thoughts with others. But if we do not develop the ability to pause and reflect, our emotions can evade the light of our intelligent reasoning.

The feelings that we are afraid to articulate are the ones that can become obsessive. When children, for example, are afraid to speak about their anger (and children do get passionately angry!), they have no outlet for their frustration. At that point they are likely to go into action, often by endangering themselves.

To express feelings like anger and jealousy in a civilized way, children need to learn that, first, it is okay to have, and talk about, them; and, second, that such feelings do not necessarily mean someone is right or good and someone is wrong or bad. Children eventually develop empathy for the other person's feelings if they have the opportunity to express their own, but only constructively and in words.

Misinformation about emotions is common. So often I hear people shame children (or themselves) for having painful or hateful feelings: "Just get over it. You shouldn't feel that way!" But emotions are as inherent a part of our biology as our need for oxygen. Often my students or patients assume I will agree that they are weak or foolish or bad for having some feeling or other. No matter how often I remind them that every feeling is normal and natural, they return to the agonized assumption that certain feelings are childish or sinful. But the fact is, everyone has all the feelings there are to have. The mind is a symphony, not a ditty, and symphonies have dark passages as well as joyful ones.

Further, what we call an "emotional problem"—such as anxiety, depression, addiction, etc.—is actually a compulsion to avoid an emotion. Addicts, for example, start out wanting to avoid some awful feeling, but then generalize to avoiding any feeling whatsoever. Inwardly they fear that opening themselves to one, even a positive one, will open them up to others. People with impulse disorders can't tolerate feeling frustrated; bullies can't tolerate feeling weak; control freaks can't tolerate feeling powerless; depressives can't tolerate feeling angry. Yet all of these intolerances vanish when sufferers are helped through reflective talk to realize they can actually survive whatever miserable feelings formerly threw them into a panic.

The emotions that people find most troublesome tend to be fear, shame, hopelessness, humiliation, impotence, loss, anxiety, hate, envy, rejection, greed, powerlessness, and inadequacy. If undiluted through reflective thinking and talking, these emotions can motivate suicide, murder, racism, war, crime, child abuse, spousal abuse, tyranny, slavery, and perhaps all the ills of mankind. Yet these perfectly ordinary, unavoidable, universal feelings and impulses are seldom spoken about comfortably in the company of others. Children enjoy participating in thoughtful discussions about puzzling behavior. For example, why did Achilles become a mass murderer? The ancient Greeks knew why—he was born of a rape (implying that his mother had conflicted feelings toward him). Children would benefit from learning that a lust for power is accompanied by an inability to love, and that many powerful leaders have been paranoid schizophrenics—Stalin, Chairman Mao, Hitler, Idi Amin, Saddam Hussein—to name a few from my lifetime. When the discussion of feelings is forbidden or belittled as a waste of time, all of us, young and old, develop self-perpetuating inhibitions. We learn to feel ashamed of being human.

The emotional centers of our mammalian brain motivate us with fear (signifying the need to protect ourselves), rage (signifying the need to counter threat, irritation, and frustration), panic (signifying separation distress, loneliness, and grief), and seeking (signifying our quest for material supplies, sex, and social contact). In addition to energizing us, our feelings inform us about our environment. Their function is to determine what is important, beneficial, meaningful, attractive, comforting, interesting, or conversely menacing or frustrating in some way. Our brain's emotional centers also decide whether something is boring, in which case we will most likely forget it.

Emotions are the central aspect of our sense of self, of our experiencing and processing the world. Primitive though they are, if the emotional parts of our brain are destroyed by injury or illness, we lose our personality, regardless of whether our cognitive centers remain perfectly intact. As has happened with some neurological patients, destruction of the emotional centers leads to complete inertia because, without feelings, nothing moves us. Without feelings we lose our ability to choose.

I find it informative to know where and how feelings are processed in our brain. One fact is well established: Our emotional centers are located separately from, and beneath, the intelligence centers in our neocortex (the top inch and a half of our brain). Designed for speed of reaction, our emotions can assess danger in a flash and react with a hair-trigger response. But when it comes to our civilized, long-range goals, our emotions can wreak havoc if we don't take the time to consult our higher cortex. Such facts should be discussed, gently and in enjoyable ways, all through school as well as at home in the family. Restraining our impulsivity is difficult if we do not develop the habit of reflecting before making choices.

Every aspect of our thinking and feeling has its purpose. Further, we cannot avoid feelings other than through binding them with neurotic, psychotic, or psychosomatic symptoms. In short the best way of managing them is through wide ranging conversation with another. Our mental health depends on this.

Also, since emotions are energy, it takes a great deal of energy to try to contain or suppress them, and we often fail if we try. In our futile struggle to contain them, we end up exhausted and frazzled. This is what we call *stress*, and stress is a cause of harmful inflammation. Further, trying to block our thoughts and feelings requires our building defenses that can ultimately distance us from reality. In short, for the sake of both our mental and physical health, we need to make peace with our emotions. It is human to think and to feel everything, and to be agonized by the conflicts that arise in this process. Only talking with a wise, knowledgeable other gives us relief. We need to talk.

B. LETTING A CHILD BE A CHILD

As children mature, they develop their own style of managing their feelings and impulses. In doing so, they are influenced by their genetic uniqueness as well as by what they have experienced and seen modeled in their environment. Some traits are actually observable in the unborn fetus: how babies respond to stimuli such as loud sounds or bright lights—whether it tends to move toward or shrink away from them, for example—is easily discerned through ultrasound. This early style of responding remains consistent after birth and on up through childhood. No two children react in exactly the same way, not even identical twins. Parenting (the same as teaching) therefore requires a lot of adjusting to accommodate the diverse personalities of both adult and child.

The infant needs a welcoming response in order to thrive. From its earliest days, the newborn seeks contact with its mother's body, voice, and eyes. It needs to see and feel her interest and her devotion. Fortunately, nature provides a hormone, oxytocin, which bonds the parent to her infant (though this depends on whether all goes well enough, which it sometimes does not.) In any case, infants lay down memory traces in the emotional centers of their brains that form their basic attitudes about the world. Is it a safe place—pleasant, reliable, and exciting? Or must the infant adapt to its being painful, harsh, or tedious? These memory traces influence all future expectations.

c. Knowing What to Expect

Each stage in the child's development places special demands on their environment. There are the needs of the one-year-old for their mother to enjoy and protect them as they start to explore their world, which at first they do by putting everything in their mouth. Hopefully their experience does not end up teaching them that their curiosity is bad and dangerous. Soon come the needs of the two-year-old, when power and independence are their passions. They are negatively suggestible, oppositional, and totally in love with saying the word "no." These maturational advances also need acceptance. Everyone should know how to get a two-year-old to eat. When they say, "No! I won't eat!" all you have to say is, "You aren't allowed to eat anything!" Then watch those little hands fly from dish to mouth. Unless the two-year-old child's use of the word "no" is welcomed, they will have difficulty saying, "yes"—possibly for the rest of their lives. The outcome of this stage permanently impacts their ability to cooperate and get along with others.

Year by year, the child's neural development introduces new strivings and needs: for vigorous play and social learning as they begin to engage in activities outside the home; for intellectual stimulation, socialization, and achievement in school; for autonomy and the beginning of the painful process of separation and individuation in their teen years. The outcomes of each stage can either enhance or damage their developing sense of self. What I notice is how often adults fear children's normal maturational strivings. For example, rare are the parents (or teachers) who encourage children to stand up to them. It may be that adults do not know how to be constructive when they try to assert themselves. Familiarity with what is normal is essential, and here is the funny thing—in truth, it is all normal. Children are incapable of being spontaneously abnormal.

Some children are more aggressive at certain stages than others; that is their nature. Yet when I hear about a toddler biting another in a daycare program, I sometimes hear the infant called "bad." The child does not know the meaning of the word, but they can hear the tone of voice in which it is uttered. But wait! We are talking about an *infant* here! Yes, they have powerful impulses when they are frustrated! But this is also normal, human functioning. They need help, not punishment. The role of the caregiver is to help them manage their impulses in a socialized way. They need to be given the words to master their experience, and the time and space in which to cool down.

"You are angry when the other child takes your toy?"

"Yes! I am angry. I am *angry!*"

"Come. Come tell me more."

Though the toddler has strong passions, they are easy to distract. A change of scene, some minutes for the powerful feelings to subside, and they are set to go. Contact and communication with the adult is balm for the pain of their frustration. End of lesson. To call them "bad" is damaging. They are not bad for having passions that they cannot yet manage on their own. The toddler's aggressive act was a signal that they were frustrated beyond their endurance—they did not yet have the ability to contain the tension of their feelings when another child grabbed something they wanted. It is the job of the caregiver to anticipate their being overwhelmed, move them out of harm's way, and help them calm down through talk and diversion.

D. RECOVERING FROM TRAUMA

My earliest recollections of being punished are laden with fear and self-loathing. Once when I was three, I was sitting at my mother's glass-topped dressing table with its china hairbrush, hand mirror, and ceramic boxes shaped like animals. I picked up a ceramic rabbit; suddenly it slipped from my fingers and shattered into bits on the floor. I felt as much as heard my mother's scream in my wildly beating heart. My father smacked my behind with the hairbrush. I didn't know what to do to fix the situation. As I describe this scene, I can still feel the thundering heartbeats of my panic, and this happened more than sixty-five years ago! Another recollection from the same period: it was Christmas, and one of my grandmother's servants offered me a piece of chocolate. I told her I wasn't allowed, but she reassured me, "Oh, it's the holiday and you can have one little piece." It melted in my mouth.

Moments later my mother saw the evidence on my lips. "You've been eating candy," she snapped. I felt as if I must disappear, vanish, be gone. But hadn't I seen her eating it? "Who gave it to you?" she demanded.

"Nobody." I knew to protect the servant.

"You're lying!" I was smacked.

A related incident: Workers were packing my toys in a barrel. We were leaving my house because my mother and father were getting something called "a divorce." I stood on my backyard swing and pumped higher and higher. I wanted to fly up and join the mynah birds squawking in the treetops. At the apex of my swing's arc I let go, my wings spread wide.

My mother was overtly trying to help me be "good"—not to touch her special things, not to eat forbidden sweets, not to tell a lie, not to be a bother. Inadvertently she also taught me something else: that my curiosity about the china figurine and my trustfulness in the servant's holiday treat were horrendous, scurrilous, monstrous acts.   I was bad for being what I was—a child.   Flooded with shame, I wanted to disappear and never bother her again. My attempt at flying was not a conscious suicide attempt—I didn't know what death was, but I wanted to get away. It was as if I was supposed to have been born knowing how to be good, and since I was not, I was unworthy to be her daughter.

I have since learned that I was not unique in feeling so awful inside when my mother screamed at me. Since children are born with their emotional centers already functioning, they sense the emotional threat in their mother's tone of voice. Genetically programmed to please her as well as to protect themselves from threat, they are willing to do so. Alas, the habit of sacrificing themselves (and feeling resentment about doing so) can turn into a lifelong trait.

Infants raised in overcrowded orphanages in third-world countries, often living in a ratio of two caregivers per sixty babies, learn not to ask for anything. But one must ask for things if one is to get by in this world. Learning not to ask has profound effects on the child's later adjustment to caregivers such as adoptive parents and teachers.

I do not blame parents. They do the best they can, despite the relentless demands of their task. The fact is that some parents are handicapped by unmet maturational needs of their own, or by stress due to illness, economic hardship, or the like. They are also influenced by the culture that surrounds them.

Meanwhile, children not only want to please and protect their parents, they also want to emulate them. I once read a study that showed that the best predictor of how far a child will go in school is how far their father went. How conflicted the child feels at the prospect of surpassing their father, all the more so if their father is emotionally distant or physically compromised! Because of the child's desire to please and protect their father, their natural competitiveness can become a knife in their own heart.

If they are depressed themselves, some parents are unable to feel or show pleasure and interest in their children. The result can be a child who inverts his natural motivation to be pleasing into its opposite. The child discovers that negative attention is better than no attention at all. In a similar vein some criminals have acknowledged that part of their motivation for breaking the law lies in their desire to be wanted (and recognized!), as in, "It is better to be wanted by the police than not to be wanted at all." This makes complete sense if we remember that the police symbolize those who control us when we are young—our parents. Additionally, criminals seek a feeling of power through their unlawful behavior. It communicates that they were unable to feel powerful just by being their loving, responsive selves as children. The motivation behind stealing is the child's belief that they are entitled to have what they need. Symbolically, thieves steal missing parental love.

Some beliefs and traditions have created conflicts for children by teaching fear and distrust of feelings. But the real question is how to socialize children without putting them into conflict with their own nature. A shy five-year-old child had a habit of pulling up her skirt to hide her face in social situations. Her mother, who wanted not to devastate her child emotionally, took her aside and tenderly explained, "It is wonderful to show your pretty body when you are in a bathing suit—like at the beach—but at a social gathering people keep their bodies covered, so that is the right thing to do. All right, darling?" Her mother helped her learn how to behave appropriately without shaming or devastating her.

E. MANAGING OUR COMPLEX HUMAN MIND

We retain thoughts, beliefs, feelings, and impulses from each stage of our development, our little child selves living on in memories that are often inaccessible to conscious recall. Inevitably we have traumas that may haunt us forever after. In a flash we can be triggered to feel once more like the scared, helpless, whiny toddler, or the stubborn, obnoxious two-year-old, or the oversexualized and rebellious teenager we once were. Our older selves pile on top of our younger selves, but still our emotional memories persist in influencing us.

A famous but cruel psychological experiment exemplifying this fact was once performed on a small baby boy who was shown a fluffy white toy rabbit as, simultaneously, a very loud bell clanged. The baby learned to respond with panic when shown anything white and fluffy. As years went by, the boy, though consciously aware that a small, white, fluffy object held no danger, continued to manifest the physiological symptoms of alarm on seeing one. It had become an unconscious emotional trigger. Such automatic reactions often emerge on the anniversary of a past trauma; variously, some feature of the current environment may arouse them. People may then feel depressed or upset without consciously knowing why, and rather focus on something in the present to create a meaning for feelings that have really to do with the past.

I often find myself dreading late autumn, when leaves turn brown and form drifts and piles in the streets. I remember once telling a therapy group I was in about how afraid I was of having the tailpipe of my car ignite them and blow up my gas tank. My chest tight with alarm,

I would obsessively kick every last leaf well out of harm's way. I urged my group mates to be very careful, too. They looked at me with puzzled expressions, but then one made a connection: "Didn't you once mention how frightened you were by the brown oak leaves when you were put in boarding school as a four-year-old?" Since I had come from tropical Hawaii, those autumn leaves epitomized my misery that year in a strange environment away from my mother and father and everything else I had ever known. My groupmate's compassion helped me connect my past with my present, abating though not altogether eradicating my tension and dread each autumn.

CHAPTER 3

ESSENTIAL EMOTIONAL FACTS TO MODEL AND TEACH

FEELINGS ARE NORMAL IMPULSES of energy that need to be expressed in safe and constructive ways, preeminently through thinking and talking. *Per se* they are neither moral nor immoral, but simply reactions to external and internal stimuli. Here I list in compact form the most important things I have learned about managing our human mind. In my view, free and open talk about them is vital. What does *not* work is to try to change them; you cannot talk yourself or anyone else out of having a powerful emotion. When we try to cheer up someone who is depressed, for example, they generally feel trivialized and more conflicted than ever:

1.Know that we are naturally ambivalent. The brain is a soft, wet structure composed of billions of nerves continuously interacting by electrical impulse, hormonal transmission, and perhaps light energy. (The physics as well as the biology of brain function is now being studied.) Like any moist container, tilt it one way to get one reaction, and tilt it another for the opposite reaction. If we have a negative feeling one moment, we may well have a positive one the next. This is not a moral issue but a biological fact. If we get stuck in a feeling, it is an indication either that a current danger is on the horizon, or that an old, painful memory has been aroused and piggybacked onto a current one. It is a good opportunity for some talk with a trusted companion or therapist to sort it out.

2. Cherish trustworthy relationships. Having emotionally friendly connections in any setting inspires us to be the best we can be, as well to stay healthy and live beyond expectations.

3. Talk and grow! Talking soothes us and simultaneously expands our mind. "A problem shared is a problem halved." Verbalization is the safest, most mature form of discharge of the energy of feelings. It leads to stress reduction, self-discovery, and inspiration. Feelings of optimism, confidence, and vitality are aroused. Talking creates new synapses in the brain, and also stimulates new brain cell growth.

4. Beware of giving advice. Though it makes us feel smart and competent to suggest solutions, it often makes the recipient feel criticized. Instead, it is most helpful to turn the other person into the expert on themselves that they alone can be. If they ask, "What should I do?" we can reply, "What would be the right choice for you?" (The right answer for us may not the right one for them. Only they know!) Plus, our consulting them about their dilemma helps them stretch their thinking and discover that they do have answers for themselves!

5. Talking restores sanity. When we talk to someone else, we not only get a discharge of the energy of whatever feeling is tying us in knots, we also gain some of the other person's state of calm. This helps restore our mental balance.

6. Act friendly regardless of what you feel. Instead of fanning the flames of an altercation, exhale deeply several times to calm down.

This is the key to having successful relationships. Emotionally we have the same brain as a dinosaur, so when we respond on purely an emotional basis, we are letting our reptilian brain take charge. To be civilized, we need to develop the habit of checking out any plan of action with our higher cortex, the part of the brain located just beneath our skull.

7. Don't tell someone to stop thinking or feeling a certain way. "Don't be angry." "Don't be sad." "Don't be afraid." Stuffing a feeling doesn't make it go away, it just drives it underground. Instead, it is therapeutic to tell someone their feeling makes complete sense, and then help them realize that nevertheless they can use their intelligence to make a decision that they can live with.

8. Get comfortable with the feeling of imperfection. Psychopathology, such as depression, results from fearing or hating something about our minds or bodies. We think, *If I weren't so stupid, pathetic, uninspired, needy, or etc., then I could succeed.* But we exhaust ourselves in vain when we try not to have such thoughts. All human beings are imperfect. In this we have no choice.

9. To get self-esteem, do estimable acts! Reaching goals is ultimately what gives us the most lasting satisfaction.

10. Protect your nervous system by limiting your amount of stimulation. Like electrical wiring, your nervous system can short circuit if overloaded. For example, an eight-year-old alarmed her mother by having a total meltdown. But the child had had way too much of a day: six hours of school, a two-hour holiday party, a one-hour after-school language class, and finally a one-and-a-half-hour evening dance class. Too much!

11. Turn your family into co-therapists. A five-year-old, excited by a coming outing, tore through the living room, overturning a lamp.

His mother ordered him to go into the other room and calm down. Moments later she heard him say, "I'm calm now. Are you calm, Mommy?" Child and mother had an agreement to discuss their states of overexcitement, and to help one another manage such moments.

12. When frustrated, children (and adults!) can build up intense aggressive energy. Know this! What, for example, are safe and effective ways of managing "road rage"? Children love being in on discussions about such dilemmas, and as they come up with answers they unwittingly train themselves to be thoughtful and deliberate.

13. Know that the human brain enjoys being destructive. Think about how naturally aggression is expressed by small children. They build a big tower of blocks and finally comes the exciting climax: boom! They knock them all down! Not once, but again and again!

14. A child's main way of expressing and managing feelings is through play. Rambunctious fun, joking around, pretending, making art, and laughing are wonderful outlets for pent-up emotional energy at any age.

15. Thoughts and feelings are not the same. The voice of reason is soft and quiet, but feelings are often loud and demanding. Civilization depends on our knowing the difference. Feelings give us valuable information, but choices of action are best when based on the outcome wanted, not merely on feelings. Children learn to exercise good judgment by being taught to anticipate and weigh all possible outcomes.

16. Keep in mind that, in the course of a child's development, learning to say the word "yes" comes after learning to say "no." Two-year-olds' favorite word is "no!" As they begin asserting their autonomy, they hate being bossed around, yet they are expected to be obedient much of each day. The problem is, our two-year-old self lives on in us. Any time we are told we must do something, our first re-

sponse is often, "No! I don't want to!" We feel powerful when we say "no!" but then we remember we want to maintain good relations with others, and finally find ourselves ready to say "yes." Conversely, we don't need to be afraid of or defeated by others' refusals. Persistence is the key to success.

17. Keep in mind what is normal and expectable in each stage of development. Adolescents, for example, want instant gratification. They need empathy as they discover they will never be the center of the universe (their most ardent desire), and that, even if they somehow get fifteen minutes of fame, it will not lead to lasting happiness.

18. Teens (and immature adults) tend to see their problems as resulting from failures of their environment, not from their own inner conflicts. "It's all *your* fault!" they shout at their beleaguered parents. A model response would be, "Well, I can't fix the past. So, what would you like me to do differently next time?" Further talk will lead the adolescent to find their own solutions.

19. Teens need adult models and mentors who make maturity look doable and enjoyable. To teens, maturity looks like a stultifying rat race. They benefit when adults appear happy with their lot in life.

CHAPTER 4

REINING IN PROVOCATIONS

A. WIN-WIN ENCOUNTERS

"**W**HY DID YOU DO THAT? What is *wrong* with you?" were the ego-lacerating questions my mother reproached me with when I made any of the careless errors a child might make. Since I was generally eager to avoid displeasing her, these questions were not designed to "remind me" or "help me learn" a new approach. (There was only one answer as to why I had erred, which was that I was human, though I had no idea that that was true as a child.) Rather, their intent was to make me feel awful, and at that they succeeded brilliantly. She snarled them in a righteous tone, possibly repeating the exact same words and tone her mother had once used with her. The outcome was that I survived my childhood and then I left home, and aside from family events and occasional letters, I chose to live far from the glare of her disapproval.

I am aware that my mother's impulse to scold me was altogether human. Our brain delights in punishing someone who frustrates us. There can even be a sexual charge to it, as famously with the Marquis de Sade. I also notice how prevalent is the belief that punishment is necessary to teach us to do the right thing—the more pain inflicted, the more powerful the lesson. This belief is built into some forms of discipline still commonly used in schools. It is not, however, what I want to do in my classroom or in my life. Though I am as prone to having sadistic impulses as anyone else, I want not to inflict them for the selfish reason that, when we are constructive with one another, life is pleasanter in the long run. So, though my reason is self-interested, everyone around me wins.

What I do when confronted with "misbehavior" is to ask a few questions to stimulate thinking. For example, a ten-year-old boy might "act up" because of a rambunctious, healthy, overabundance of energy. In this case, his affect will not be sullen or oppositional, but still it can prove out of place in the classroom or at a social gathering. The most constructive option is to help him express some of that energy in rambunctious, energetic talk. I might take a moment to ask, "Looks like you're feeling full of oats. Want to tell me about it?"

Since feelings are the core of the child's vulnerable sense of self, they can only be revealed if the child feels safe. When children have tried to provoke me over the years, I have come to realize that they are usually testing me. They want to know whether I will react in a way that confirms their view that adults are angry despots. Expecting it, they relieve their tension by getting it out into the open, and over and done with. If I react in a negative way, their distrust is reinforced. Only by not reacting negatively can I be effective.

On the first day of a new term, a teenager came into my class wearing a headset pounding out the beat of rap music. The tension in his body and his avoidance of eye contact signaled that he was primed for confrontation. I respected him by saying nothing for a while, just going about introducing myself to the class, taking attendance, and the like. But every so often I would move closer to him and gently urge, "You've got to put that away now." His response each time was to twist his upper body away from mine with a fierce jerk. Finally he yanked the headset off and screamed, "It doesn't matter if I'm bad or good, you'll still be angry at me!"

As is my custom, I did not show a hint of dismay, though my heart was beating wildly. The boy never wore his headset again, nor would he let any of his classmates wear theirs. Also, he never again presented a hint of provocation in my classroom. Clearly, this child was telling me the story of his whole life, first with his behavior and then with his words. It is self-evident that the important adults in his past had been chronically angry with him! Exercising my customary, professional self-control, I freed him to tell me what had been tormenting his mind. The outcome, his becoming cooperative thereafter, showed how much he benefited from just that one dose of understanding.

Class went on normally after the scene, as if it had never taken place, though I suspect that his classmates were reverberating inside from his intensity, as I certainly was, and wondering about what they had witnessed. As usual, while it seemed I was interacting with only the one child, I was actually interacting with them all. Eventually, after they had been with me for a while, they would tell me their belief that I could talk a mugger out of mugging me. Such comments showed that they did indeed notice the powerful effect of my acting in an unflappably soothing, and rational way.

I demonstrated that feelings such as sadism (naturally my first impulse) could be managed constructively. What a dramatic and important lesson for them! Cautiously, I had made sure not to approach too close to the headset boy lest he lose what modicum of self-control he may have possessed. I am not a martyr or a fool. Though I have never once had to use it in all my years of teaching in the inner city, I always keep my escape route ready to mind.

Pretending to be reliably calm is a powerful response to someone who is in an agitated state. Not just this headset-wearing boy, but innumerable others during my teaching career, tested me with similar dramas. When they were responded to with quiet dignity and interest rather than punitiveness, they calmed down and ultimately became cooperative, as the headset wearer had done. By not reacting to their provocativeness in kind, I reversed their underlying distrust. I am careful never to expose even an edge in my voice or a twinge of dismay on my face. Children's defiance and desire to defeat the teacher only increases if he or she reacts to it with fear or anger.

Even aside from the extreme cases, I know that it is natural for my students to want to defeat me. As a residue of our "terrible twos," we are all negatively suggestible to some degree. No sooner do we hear the rules than we want to break them. This is reflected in the joke about the mother who, reading her children the riot act before leaving them home alone, tried to cover every base. She finally added, "And whatever you do, don't stuff beans up your nostrils." We all know what her kids did—or wanted to do—the moment the door closed behind her. But if a teacher remains unruffled in the face of hostility, the spiteful fun of it deflates. Her quietness helps their underlying desire for connection to resurface. Having had their moment of manic excitement, the students revert to wanting to please her.

Daniel, a short, dark-haired boy who looked closer to twelve than his actual age of fifteen, was one of a number of middle-class youngsters who enrolled in the alternative high school where I spent my final years of teaching. He, too, came to us after being expelled from a previous high school, in his case a prestigious private one. I initially had him in a writing course. Though he did not dress in a hip-hop style of some of the inner city youngsters, his face was as sullen and unsmiling as the toughest of theirs. By the end of the first week, he had distinguished himself by not handing in a single assignment. Furthermore, he would not speak. In the second week he actually handed in a paper, but all it had on it was his name. I returned it to him the following day with an "A+" and watched him glance at it without the least change of expression.

The following day I taught a lesson on "brainstorming"—the process of jotting down as many ideas as possible on a topic before writing an actual essay. My plan was to generate a list and then sort it into related themes that could be developed into paragraphs. Mindful to use something of interest to adolescents, I chose "Causes of Car Accidents." After some introductory remarks, I wrote the topic on the chalkboard and opened the floor for contributions. The students began with the more obvious ones: "icy streets, faulty brakes, speeding, giant potholes," and I listed them on the board. One well-dressed boy observed that not all accidents are the driver's fault, and told an anecdote about how he himself had hit and killed a drunken pedestrian late one rainy night. "It was the drunk's fault," he insisted. Moreover, the drunk had left an imprint of tooth marks on his car's hood, and he felt both annoyed and guilty seeing this reminder every day. I added "drunken pedestrians" to the chalkboard list.

At this point Daniel raised his hand for the first time ever and offered a contribution: "Hemorrhoids." The flatness in his tone of voice effectively masked what he was up to, and I wrote it on the board. He proceeded to flood me with others in the same vein— "anal fissures; rectal bleeding; flatulence; fistulas; proctitis; rectal prolapse; fecal incontinence; rectal warts," and I listed them as fast as I could write. Daniel's deadpan tone never wavered, and no one else in the class batted an eye. Finally I could hold it in no longer: I burst out laughing. When the bell rang moments later, the class walked out as calmly and coolly as if nothing out of the ordinary had transpired. And that is how I made friends with Daniel.

Well, not exactly *friends*—though he began enrolling in other classes with me, he kept himself at a cautious distance. Still, his facial expression grew more relaxed, and I sometimes noticed him laughing and chatting with other students instead of holding himself aloof, as had been his habit. When he vanished one day, I learned from his adviser that he had reconciled with his father and returned to his old school. I credit myself for his softening his "shut-down" stance, thereby enabling him to patch things up with his father. What had worked? I believe it was just my accepting his need to be defiant. I suspect that his father had failed to understand Daniel's adolescent need to establish his autonomy by being oppositional, but I never did find out whether his father was a proctologist or a long-suffering victim of rectal problems.

B. Using My Students As My Consultants

When my students bring to my attention the fact that they have not done something constructive that they claimed they wanted to do, I usually ask (without a trace of criticism in my tone), "What stopped you from doing it?" Some try to shuffle off the task of answering onto me: "You're the expert. You tell me."

"Now, wait a minute," I reply. "*You* are the only real expert on yourself, so what good would my guess be?"

At this point they are stymied. They love hearing that they are experts on themselves, and after only a moment's thought realize it is true. At the same time, the child in them wants to force the adult in me to take responsibility. I empathize—it can be hard to know why we make bad decisions or fail to make good ones. It is much easier for teens to blame adults, which they typically do. But ultimately who will take care of them if they do not learn to do it themselves? Hillel, in 30 B.C., said it best: "If I cannot rely on myself, on whom can I rely?" We all know the answer is "no one." To adolescents, adulthood looks unattainable. Their brains are not ready to take on the task, however much their hormones insist. One minute they feel and act like exhausted infants; the next they are wild with passion. They cannot help being teenagers, and they still need a great deal of attention and guidance, just as smaller children do.

One of my colleagues once scolded me for spending a few class minutes interacting with an obstreperous child. She felt I should simply have demanded that he be quiet and get back on task. To her, my interest in establishing an emotional connection was a time-wasting diversion. However, nowadays I can cite business management theory that teaches that even adult employees perform best when they feel understood by their bosses. Authorities of any kind are wise to keep this in mind. I also know that children cannot grow up fast, regardless of circumstances forcing them to. They may go through the motions, but inside they remain impoverished. I see a major part of my job as giving them the missing emotional experiences needed for them to feel secure and accepting of themselves, to whatever extent I can.

A concern I often hear is that the rest of the class will get unruly or bored as I interact with one class member (or cluster). This has never been my experience. Rather, the other students stare in fascination. Many identify with whomever I am consulting, at least to some extent. Instead of reaching only the one student, I actually reach them all, demonstrating an invaluable model of emotional intelligence as well as compassion and concern.

But suppose a whole class did become disorderly, something like a gang? I have known whole groups to do this, particularly around holidays such as Halloween or before vacation breaks. Keeping in mind that their inner desire is to connect with me, I remain silent but calmly alert. I know within a minute or two they will take notice of my motionlessness. I have seen this work with unruly groups of all ages, including special education children. Sooner or later, one stops and glances at me, and then the others fall silent, too, one by one. That is when I consult them: "Looks like something's going on. Any idea what it is?"

Having gotten a bit of patience, interest, and concern from me, they may tell me what is on their minds. "Buzz buzz buzz"—all of them want to contribute. The hidden benefit of this approach is that they feel respected as I simply listen, and then are inspired to be respectful in turn. So what if it takes a couple of minutes? The resulting quality of the students' attention more than pays off when I return to my lesson. What a change from my earliest years of teaching when I tried to control my students through coercion. I would feel exhausted and defeated, and my nerves would feel jangled for the rest of the day.

c. A Contractual Relationship

I find it helpful to begin a semester by talking with my students about the contract we have together. Not all children understand that getting a grade is part of a contract, so I initiate an interview that goes something like this: "What would you like to get from this class?" The most frequent response from my inner-city students was "a passing grade."

"Would you like to know how to get it?"

"Yes," they would reply tentatively, uncertain what I was up to.

I kept it simple: "Here's how: Maintain minimum attendance; do all homework and class work; and pass all tests." I also added that they were to help one another cooperate and learn.

Many students would not take me at my word. It made me wonder if they had suffered broken promises in the past, or had somehow learned that failure is the only way to get attention. Or perhaps they had learned that, with a little seductiveness, they could get whatever they wanted? In any event, the way some approached me at the end of the marking period showed they had not believed me. "How come you failed me?" they would ask.

"I thought you liked me!" some would add, sounding genuinely hurt.

"Of course I like you!" I would exclaim. It made me think that, at home, in their first school, they had learned that rules didn't matter so long as they could induce guilt in their parents. But such seductions are not how reality works, and I wanted to teach them this emotional fact of life. "What does my liking you have to do with anything? I like you whether you pass or fail!" I would say. I love to get dramatic, so I would often add, "As a matter of fact, I think it would be wonderful if you failed for the next ten years so you could stay with me until I'm ready to retire!" Interestingly, some part of me honestly felt that way! But I also knew that failure in school is a child's favorite way of getting back at their parents, so I made it perfectly clear that their failure was not going to dismay me (the symbolic parent). At no time did I use a sarcastic tone of voice, for that would only make them revert to think-ing of me as the enemy and of grades as idiosyncratic sadism on my part.

"Then why did you fail me?" they would pursue. Some of them really did not get it.

I would open my roll book and point out absences and/or missed assignments, sounding as surprised as they by the evidence: "Let's see . . .It looks like I didn't get this—and this—and oh, yes, look at these attendance figures!" This style of interaction hits on a number of emotional facts of life. I have already mentioned students' negative suggestibility, but there is another powerful dynamic that is concealed in failure: Children sometimes need to fail as a way to cope with intolerable feelings, for example in reaction to a family breakup. It is not done with clear, conscious planning. Still, the important thing is that when the teacher does not react with a scolding or a sign of dismay, the child's gratification in defeating them (as symbolic of the parent) through their failure is nullified.

In place of anger and/or harsh, punitive reactions, there are strategies that will not be experienced as negative by the child. I spoke above about consulting a child as to what is stopping them from attending to the contract. Sometimes just getting something off their chest will help them settle down. If it is too embarrassing to speak in front of the class, the child could be invited to write a note to the teacher. Perhaps if the child sits right next to the teacher this might help (or the very prospect may be so appalling that this question gets them to reconsider their behavior.) Would the child like some time out to calm down? (Perhaps the teacher has a colleague who could take them for a few minutes). If a child remains out of control, the teacher could pull out the ultimate weapon by asking, "Should I have the thought of sending you to the dean?" The teacher is only voicing a thought, yet this is precisely what the child dreads most—the teacher's having a negative thought about them! I have seen children recoil with hurt and dismay just because I expressed the possibility of having such a thought about them—they needed so much to be liked.

The wonderful thing about consulting children is that it stimulates them to reflect. The dean will almost never need to be called, and everyone in the room will get another valuable demonstration of how to think about and handle difficult feelings.

There were only two occasions during my entire career when I had to take the extreme measure of sending for a dean, both of which involved a child's use of violence. My cardinal rule, which any student of mine could recite, was that talking was the only behavior allowed in my room (aside from schoolwork, which goes without saying). On the first occasion, an ordinarily nice teenager named Paul suddenly upended a heavy piece of furniture with a great crash. Though no one got hurt, I didn't even stop to think as I dashed out into the hall shouting for a guard. Later, Paul confided to me why he had done it: "I wanted to act crazy because nobody messes with a crazy person." His action had been a deliberate communication to another child who, unbeknownst to me, had menaced him. I remember then rather admiring Paul's choice; he had been protecting himself by deliberately putting on an act. Though with it he demonstrated his potential for violence, he did not actually hurt anyone, nor had he intended to. He later told me that he had used the same tactic on an earlier occasion in his neighborhood, also to great success. He repeated his observation to me that no one, not even gang members, wants to deal with a madman.

The second occasion I called a dean was when a quiet but obviously smoldering boy spun an empty wastepaper basket across the room at me so that it barely missed grazing my knee. I actually was at fault. I had been grilling the boy about his attendance, miscalculating how this was a humiliation beyond his tolerance. We eventually made up, but I regret that blunder to this day. One look at him should have been enough to tell me how badly he needed his pride to be protected.

D. When More Extreme Strategies Are Needed

If a child was chronically out of control, a real hard case, I would ask, "Should I get someone to help you control yourself? Perhaps a parent or a volunteer might sit by you in the classroom for a while?" I saw this work a miracle with James, a hyperactive teenager who had driven every teacher in the alternative school into despair. I had begun working with him individually, ostensibly to give him help with his reading, though another important goal was to give his teachers a break. We worked cozily together for a while, but after several weeks James announced that he didn't want to meet alone with me anymore. Instead, he asked that I come sit next to him in his science class. I asked him what I would do there, and he informed me that he didn't want me to talk to him or help him with his work—just to sit there near him. Because I have great respect for anyone's self-prescription, I gave it a try. After explaining the plan to James's science teacher, I found a seat near him and sat down. James would turn to look at me from time to time, but he did all his work on his own. There was not a hint of his former agitated behavior. When other students in his class asked me for help, I patiently told them I couldn't give it because I was there for James. I would note that James turned to look at me each time he heard me say those words. As if by magic, James became a model student in all his classes. Had he never had anyone devote herself to him before in his life? Was this the missing "emotional nutrient" James needed? The evidence suggests this is so.

When options such as, "Would you like someone to sit with you and help you concentrate?" are offered in a friendly voice, the child is baffled. Where is the shaming and the punishment they expected? How can they keep on being oppositional and hateful to a teacher who is being patient and affable? I have also seen a classmate step forward to help such a child. The attitude to be conveyed is that we all need help controlling ourselves from time to time, another invaluable life lesson.

E. Humor Helps!

Not long ago I was invited to consult with the maintenance staff of a day hospital program for severely mentally ill patients. One problem presented to me was that an old-time staff member was making a certain new staff member feel miserable. No different from siblings, old-timers get jealous and resentful when a new hire comes on board. This came to a boil in one meeting when the old staff member kept jumping out of his seat to emphasize the inadequacies of the recently hired coworker (who sat tensely across the room). "Sit down!" I ordered, but he kept bouncing up to add, "And another stupid thing he does is. . ."

So I leapt up too, saying, "If you do that again I am going to have a heart attack and faint right here on the floor. I will probably have convulsions and foam at the mouth, and I may soil my underwear right here on this spot!" The old hiree looked startled, perhaps appalled, but he sat down and finally fell quiet. I had used a technique called "out-crazying the crazy," which often works when nothing else will. At a following meeting the old staff member told me he had made friends with the new one.

I like to have fun. It stimulates the opiods in my brain, at one and the same time calming me and giving me pleasure. Another teacher once told me his tactic of approaching an unruly child in a hallway and saying in a confidential voice, "You know, if you keep this up, I'm going to have to call my mother in to interview you, and you will *not* like being interviewed by my mother, because she only has two teeth and they're both very rotten, and her breath smells so bad you can tell when she's coming from a mile away!" How creative! The child walks away not feeling attacked, but helps to control themselves in this goofy way that is ridiculous and funny and sort of feels good.

F. LET'S NOT BRUISE KIDS' EGOS

Here is an anecdote told to me by a guidance counselor that illustrates how desperately children need help managing their destructive impulses and feelings, especially when the regular teacher is absent.

It seems a fourth-grade class had a substitute teacher. Predictably, by mid-afternoon the children began to get restless. Out of the blue one little girl erupted in screaming hysterics. The story that haltingly came out through her sobs was that a boy had whispered to another boy that he'd like to pull her panties down and take a peek, and that the second little boy had told this to her. The substitute teacher, understandably upset, called the principal, who immediately called the boys' parents and announced that he was suspending their sons from school for a week. The boys' parents had to take costly days off from work to come in for hearings. The girl's father, a police officer with a gun prominently strapped on his hip, shouted at the guidance staff, "Something has to be done about this, and I mean now!" The stress from this expanding drama upset a lot of people for many weeks.

Children need their teachers to be knowledgeable and comfortable with the emotional facts of life, and not to be shocked by their feelings and impulses. They depend on adults to help them grow up. It is to be expected that children will get out of control when they have a substitute teacher. It is also to be expected that boys will have sexual impulses and to want to tease girls. An alternative to creating a major crisis such as in this case would be to call a time out for cooling down, and then conduct a class discussion/debriefing along the lines of: "You know, it's hard having a substitute teacher, and that is probably what caused this incident." (Now feeling safe and understood, the little boys would return to their rational minds.) "But it resulted in some strong feelings for this young lady." (And the little girl would feel understood, and safer, and calmer.) "Could we talk about the feelings when there is a substitute teacher?" (With this question, all of the children would feel understood. They have no clear idea of why they feel unruly impulses when they have a substitute teacher.)

After listening to the group tell her how mean they feel inside when their regular teacher is absent, the substitute can explore a little further: "So is it okay to tease a girl and hurt her feelings or frighten her? Do you want her to hate you or like you?" With this approach the children will learn many valuable lessons: that their often frightening impulses can be talked about, that others have them too, and that they feel much better if they are not demonized for misbehavior but rather encouraged to do some thinking before repeating them.

While children enjoy the thrill of provoking excitement, they are also frightened and dismayed by their unruly urges. When overstimulated, they realize that things can escalate to dangerous levels. They may momentarily resent having the teacher interrupt and calm them down through talk, but they will also feel relieved. Children have a number of feelings at any moment, so why not emphasize the saner ones?

An informed emotional approach is useful with graduate students, too. A professor consulted me about a class of doctoral candidates who were acting in a hostile and competitive way with one another, as well as criticizing the professor. Understandably the students were desperate to complete their dissertations after their years of intense study, but their squabbling truly shocked the instructor, who had impulses to abandon the class. After empathizing with the professor, I gave her some suggestions about how to calm her students' agitation. First, she could acknowledge their feelings, which of course were understandable. After all, who does not want to murder a competitor? Then she could consult with them about whether their goal was to write a quality paper or to have a race to the finish. Though they probably want both, just thinking through that question would sober them up. The professor could then add a group goal, to wit, that their task was to write their papers and help one another do the same.

G. MANAGING COMPLAINTS, CRITICISMS, AND HOSTILITY

The fact that I recommend never responding in a critical or hostile way is the most unnatural part of my approach. I have even been called dishonest for it. In truth I often feel rage or pain at some of the things my students, colleagues, and even family members do and say, and I have the impulse to tell them a thing or two. But as a knowledgeable adult, I have other, quieter feelings, as well. I have empathy when they are so filled with anger. Often they are not even aware how confrontational they are being! I do not want to add to their emotional traumas. I do want to help them grow emotionally. So I am not being inauthentic but just choosing which of my feelings I put into action. Those who say unfriendly things are at war with themselves. There would be no point in adding to their distress other than satisfying an impulse for revenge. Also, I know that how I handle my own responses is crucial to gaining their trust.

Here is an anecdote about a fifteen-year-old and a new teacher: Jenny was a freshman in a new school where she found the amount of homework daunting. She was also suffering intense personal anguish due to her parents' battling their way through a prolonged and acrimonious divorce. When her health teacher gave her class a lengthy report to write, Jenny objected: "Health Class is only a one-credit course, so why such a big assignment? It's ridiculous!" The teacher responded by ridiculing Jenny's protest, making her fury skyrocket. She tried first to organize her classmates into boycotting the assignment and then into failing the class *en masse*, believing that this would force the principal to fire the health teacher. Meanwhile she could hardly think about anything else. (It may be that this incident provided a welcome distraction from what was going on at home.) Though she ultimately did the assignment, she only gave it a lukewarm effort, when she was perfectly capable of achieving an "A."

Now, what if the teacher had consulted Jenny about her complaint? The teacher could have said, "Have I made the assignment too difficult?"

Jenny would have said, "Yes!" and at once have felt better.

The teacher could then have continued the consultation: "Is there any way I can help you to do it? Should we do part of it in class together?"

Despite their unruly impulses, children, as biologically sociable beings, also always want to please their caregivers. Though in adolescence this civilized desire can be eclipsed by the teens' need for establishing a sense of independence, it is still lying in wait somewhere inside their minds. Students benefit from having clear expectations and gentle reminders about what is wanted from them. They benefit from offers of help. Further, if the teacher views a child's breaking a rule as a nonverbal communication and then helps the child use their words rather than actions to say it, the child is not only grateful but wants to attach to and emulate the teacher. Their motivation to please is rekindled. This strengthens them emotionally. As their feelings cool down, the children sort themselves out and redirect their energies. This, and not knee-jerk obedience, is the essence of maturation. To boot, the teacher is spared the impossible task of trying to force them to do something they refuse to do.

However, I do have my limits. When someone complains that I have been remiss, their accusatory tone of voice can still stimulate me to doubt myself and then to crave revenge. Here are the thoughts that help me regain my sanity and composure:

I cannot fix backwards. Therefore, there is no point in feeling defensive (doubting or hating myself) about any mistake I might have made. Instead, as the C.E.O. of myself, I give myself executive permission to be imperfect. If I am feeling playful, as I do a lot of the time, I entertain myself thinking of retorts like, "So sue me!" which I may or may not express, given the circumstances.

I can fix forward. This is best done by turning the person whom I have offended into a consultant on their own feelings: "What would you like me to do about this?" Then I listen to their answer. If they want an apology, I usually give it. Most of all, I listen seriously, and in my experience this is usually enough.

A complainer needs confirmation that their feelings make sense. To them, they always do (though of course, so do mine to me). Conveying this understanding is a constructive way to handle any confrontation. I can do it with a sympathetic nod, the neutral statement,

"I hear you," or just calm silence. Alternately, I can do something we therapists call "joining"—saying something that agrees with the other's point of view, whether in reality I actually do or do not.

My sister once consulted me because my mother, who was visiting her, was in a state of great agitation. My mother was certain that my sister had insulted her by seating her next to the chef at a dinner party. In truth my sister was honoring my mother by doing this—the chef was renowned for her cookbooks and newspaper columns on food, and was her longtime friend and neighbor! My mother, however, could only see that she had been belittled. She had been up all night agonizing about it, and her blood pressure was spiking dangerously.

I gave my sister a "joining" strategy to use, meaning a communication that would calm my mother down and help her regroup: "Tell her, 'It looks like I've been a bad daughter.'"

"But I didn't do anything wrong!" my sister protested.

I gave her a brief explanation and urged her on: "Just try it!" So she did.

"Yes, that's right! *Now* you understand," my mother had sighed, ending her tears. When it comes to overheated emotional states, there is no truth or justice—just an out-of-control situation that needs managing. While a reality-based response almost never works, joining always does.

CHAPTER 5

MIRRORING NARCISSUS

A. The Human Need for Interest and Admiration

THE ANCIENT GREEKS DEMONSTRATED their ability to observe mental disturbance in their mythology. The story of Narcissus, in particular, portrays the injury that can result from a mother's negative feelings about a child. Narcissus, a handsome adolescent, was so preoccupied with his self-image as reflected on the surface of a pond that he neglected to attend to anything else. In time he died of starvation and exposure to the elements. The motivation for his suicidal passivity is given in a detail given at the beginning of the myth: Narcissus was born of a rape. The implication is that his mother did not welcome his birth and so was unable to give him the devoted interest and nurturance needed to bring him to life. An infant with a rejecting mother sustains a traumatic injury to the development of their sense of self. Rather it was as if Narcissus was missing a sense of self, hence his urgent searching of his reflection in the water.

My mother, my first teacher, never developed much beyond her own narcissism, though she was quite capable of criticizing it in me. "Stop thinking about yourself so much," she would say dismissively when I tried to get her attention. Her message was clear: "Leave me alone." I could not know she had been traumatized herself. As a teenager, I was desperate for her recognition and affirmation. With my biological father four thousand miles away in Hawaii, she was the focus of my inner life, the one whom I considered important above all others. Like all children, I blamed myself for my failure to win her interest or admiration.

Aside from flattening my self-esteem, my mother was a good mother. I felt taken care of by her in the basics. We lived a safe, predictable life—three healthy meals a day, semi-annual visits to the dentist, our inoculations always up to date. I knew I would not get the same care if I lived with my biological father. As a teenager I was aware that my impulsivity, particularly with boys, could get me into serious trouble. I needed my mother's restrictions. She could not help me feel like a star, but safety was more important than my self-esteem, since at that time my alarm system never stopped ringing.

B. ADDRESSING UNMET NARCISSISTIC NEEDS

I see many human problems as stemming from unmet narcissistic needs in infancy and childhood. When the baby does not find enough loving interest in their mother's eyes, they become desperate. Inside they feel unfocused and empty. Most often they end up turning their anger against themselves or actively exposing themselves to danger. Children need to store up memories of loving responses from their caregivers, both to inspire them to prosper in the future, and to survive the unhappy moments they suffer in the present.

C. A THERAPEUTIC APPROACH TO NARCISSISM

Studying my own narcissism, I notice how I always start by seeing others from the template of myself. If I am feeling shy, I assume the other feels shy, too. Studying my responses helps me know how to initiate a relationship with others. If I respect their narcissistic needs, I will gain their confidence. I know to ask a friendly question or two, act interested in their answers (after a while, I become interested for real), and we generally establish a connection.

The scene is a cocktail party, time to meet and greet—a difficult prospect for me, as I am shy. But I approach a stranger and ask a low-keyed question: "So what brought you to this party?" and follow up with further mild curiosity: "How long have you known the host?" Usually I discover something that the two of us have in common. Intrigued by finding ways that we mirror each other, we pursue our conversation with growing ease. I use this technique with friends, relatives, patients, students, social contacts, taxi drivers—everyone. I do it out of self-interest. I know people are at their best when they feel they are with someone who is like them—a kind of mirror. I will get better service, better follow-through, a warmer response. Often it leads to some fun—a surprising anecdote or joke that brightens my day.

A therapist friend told me a story of the wonderful gift he received after doing an "intake" (a therapeutic interview such as I described above) with a cab driver who was taking him to a funeral. The cabbie responded by sharing some aspects of his life back home in Guyana, but then sympathetically asked, "Whose funeral are you attending?" When my friend replied that a beloved elderly relative had died, the cabbie quoted an expression in his native French: *"Quand un vieux mouri, une libraire est brouleé."* ("When an old person dies, a library goes up in flames!") What a profound and truthful way to express the enormity of a loss.

I once served as a consultant to a group of counselors whose job was to help inner-city teen mothers in a recovery program for substance abuse. I recall a problem they had on "Graduation Day": When a counselor called a girl up to the podium and offered some brief, admiring comments about her, the nongraduates in the audience muttered audibly, "*What?* That counselor could say those same things about me!" By creating these disturbing distractions, the nongraduates were revealing their distress that the spotlight was not on them. Such immature behavior is expectable with narcissistic people; what these young women were conveying was their starvation for attention. As always, a reprimand would only have exacerbated their distress. Best would be to arrange positive moments for them as the others graduated, the way we might provide a gift for the siblings of a birthday boy.

Narcissism can be a major barrier to relationships. It makes us predict that others will be similar to us, and when they are not, we often lose interest. Not long ago my husband had an "aha" experience in this regard. A nurse checking his vital signs during a medical visit asked what he did for a living. When he replied that he was an artist, she seemed to brighten up with interest. Assuming at once that she was an art lover, he began to describe his latest work. Whatever she said next indicated a total lack of an art background, and his interest in her vanished as quickly as it had appeared. Through revealing her differentness, she lost her meaning for him. His bubble of narcissism burst.

I capitalize on my knowledge of the dynamics of human narcissism by not revealing personal information about myself to my students or patients. Sooner or later they may press me: "Are you married? Do you have any children? How old are you? What is your nationality or racial background? Have you ever used drugs?" I reply by inviting them to guess. Often the question my inner-city high school students were most interested in was what I "got high" on, and when I said, "Guess!" they of course revealed their own preferences. If at length they pressed me hard enough, I would tell them the truth: "I get high on working with you!" Not only was this true, it strengthened their narcissistic bond with me.

Most of my relationships are with people who mirror my interests in some way. My strongest connections are with those who share my genes, though family relationships, too, can founder due to narcissistic differences. My two closest friends are psychotherapists with whom I have been meeting bi-monthly in a "peer group" for thirty years. We are close in age, share professional dilemmas, are growing old together, and can tell one another our most private thoughts with complete abandon. Any time one of us is in distress, our first impulse is to call the other two, for we know we will get the support we need without any of the platitudes or competitiveness common to most social inter-change. Among the three of us there is collectively over ninety years of clinical experience. Yet it is the sense of trust in each other that is most significant.

After almost fifty years of marriage, my husband is my rock, and I am his. Like other senior citizens, when we walk down the street holding hands, it is not so much romance as an attempt to prevent one another from tripping and falling on our faces. This we find funny. We can laugh now at one another's foibles, knowing neither of us is or ever will be perfect. Many of our interests are different, but in the important things we are a narcissistic match: We like to eat the same foods, engage in the same recreations, fuss over our pets, dote on our grandchildren, and laugh at the ridiculousness of being human. We're both conservative with money and uninterested in a glitzy life style. When we are upset or frightened, we cling together like limpets on a rock. We love each other but have grown comfortable hating each other, too. For example, I hate him because there is the possibility that he might predecease me. Since we have agreed to keep our hating feelings to ourselves, our life together is a haven.

D. Narcissism and Cultural Difference

Exposure to cultural difference is frightening and disorienting to a child. As a little girl, when I visited my grandmother, I noted how her servants were of a different ethnic and cultural background. Though I loved and trusted them and played with their children as equals, I nonetheless took on my family's attitude of their being some-how less than we were—this despite the fact that I preferred being with them in my grandmother's big, bustling kitchen to sitting near my grown-ups sipping their cocktails and shushing me. I also preferred their savory ethnic food to my family's blander roast beef. But I knew not to express my preference for being with them to my family members. It created a sort of racism in me that was really an anxiety that, if I didn't sound the way my tribe did, I would be in danger of being exiled. I now know this is a common childhood fear, but I had no perspective on it back then.

When I was twenty years old I attended the University of Madrid's summer program, held in the northwestern coastal town of Santander. I spent most afternoons sunning on the beach and swimming in the cold waters of the Atlantic Ocean. A handsome, courtly teenager named Felix began to visit with me each day, and I struggled to speak Castilian Spanish (distinguished by a stylish lisp) with him. My romantic fantasy was that he came from an aristocratic local family. After a week or so, he invited me to meet him at a local club one evening, and I happily accepted. When I got there, I was startled to find his entire family with him. I knew that unmarried Spanish women were chaperoned on a date, but I had never heard the same was true for young men. Felix introduced me to his siblings and their spouses as we joined them at their table. There was live music and dancing in the background, making my struggles to communicate in my halting Spanish more difficult than ever. Unexpectedly, another young man, a stranger, tapped me on the shoulder and invited me to dance. In the custom of back home in America, I danced with him to one tune before sitting back down with Felix. However, by doing so I apparently committed a gross indiscretion, for after that evening Felix never spoke to me again.

As an adult I want to expand beyond such painful limitations. Since my tyrannical grandmother is gone, and my mother and her siblings are gone, my generation of cousins and our offspring have married people with different nationalities, ethnicities, religions, skin colors, and social strata. These differences that would have shocked my grandmother to her bones, and my mother and her siblings as well, are perfectly acceptable to the rest of us.

E. NARCISSISM AND MURDER

Many wars and injustices have been based on people acting out the shock and revulsion they feel in the face of others who appear to be different. We feel ill at ease with people who are not our mirrors in appearance, in customs, even in the sports teams they champion. Conversely, we feel at home among those who vote for the same political candidate and see the world's problems and solutions the same way we do.

Dissimilarity can make children feel painful doubt ("Maybe I am the weird one") or fear ("You talk funny!") They assume that the one who appears "different" feels the same way toward them. Children need the opportunity to discuss this dilemma freely, including the feelings of envy or hatred or disgust or superiority that are aroused. To condemn such normal responses only forces them underground, there to lie in wait for an opportunity to spring into action. This is yet another reason not to scold children (or adults!) for having narcissistic feelings, but rather to help them hold thoughtful discussions about them.

f. Narcissism in the Inner-City Classroom

The impact of generations of poverty and despair on families living in the inner city is enormous. A New York Times article (January 24, 2007) entitled "Childhood Poverty Is Found to Portend High Adult Costs" estimated that "children who grow up poor cost the economy $500 billion a year because they are less productive, earn less money, commit more crimes, and have more health-related expenses." Poverty in the inner city can be a self-perpetuating life style with a culture of its own, especially given that those with middle-class aspirations flee to better neighborhoods as fast as they can. For this reason, helping inner-city children cope with their privations and fears is crucial to their success in life. Without the help of informed adults, they can be locked into patterns of despair.

As I have noted, self-attack is the most common way that children manage anger and desperation. Frequently they do this through risky behavior such as substance abuse, failure in school, unprotected sex, and committing crimes. Living in a milieu of others as desperate and despairing as they reinforces their behavioral patterns. Anyone middle class is viewed as an outsider and therefore suspect. They even see school as "middle class" and therefore alien (not a narcissistic mirror). My inner city students used to tell me that doing well in school is "white." Underlying this attitude are not only their feelings of inadequacy, but also their fear that becoming educated would constitute a betrayal of their family and milieu.

In their narcissistic discomfort they feel suspicious about connecting with the teacher. Nonetheless, they all yearn to be tamed and loved. I have found this to be true with even the most hardened "bad" kid. In order to expand beyond the models of their familiar milieu, they need a relationship with a wise and knowledgeable adult who can encourage them by providing a new, reliable and caring model to admire and emulate.

g. Ego Insulation as the Antidote to Narcissism

Children (like adults!) are vulnerable to humiliation and psychic pain. We psychotherapists call such experiences "narcissistic hemorrhages," the abrupt emptying out of every good feeling as shame and worthlessness flood their sensorium. Children can only outgrow their vulnerability to narcissistic hemorrhaging if they get sufficient success and recognition stored in their memory banks. Self-esteem is mainly built on what Alcoholics Anonymous calls "estimable acts," though there must be someone there to witness them. This is why having a family member who takes notice of the child's efforts to do well is so vital (though teachers, too, can contribute). Whenever we find something to appreciate about a child, we add a valuable input to their mind. Later, such positive memories and feelings are available to insulate their ego and neutralize their current suffering. This is another biological basis of mental health and therapeutic change.

Knowing that everyone on this planet is narcissistic, I consider it beneficial to mirror anyone with whom I interact. The purpose is to help them feel safe with me so that they are less likely to be distracted by such thoughts as, She is nothing like me, so why should I give a damn about her? It is when people feel "at home" that communication is most open and at ease. As I have noted above, I do not reveal personal data, for that could destroy the fantasy of me as a narcissistic mirror. If they question me about my background, I mirror by questioning, "What is your thought?" If pressed about my ethnic background, again I say, "Guess!" But eventually I might tell them a reassuring truth: "I am a mutt—a little bit of everything." Thus, I find it is actually possible to mirror everyone! I also make use of their expressions and gestures as another way to mirror them. One student cozily introduced me to her mother, "This is my teacher, Sheila. She's white outside, but inside she's black like us!"

Another important tactic I use is to try to find something uniquely endearing about each child. With one it might be a talent for humor, with another graphic skills, with another an interest in food, or a way of tying his shoelaces, or musical talent, athleticism, hairdo, ability to suck his teeth in disgust, and so forth. One of my students could sneeze louder than anyone I had ever met and was always delighted when I took notice of it. Observing me picking up on these things about them, my students often urged me to go around the classroom and say something I had observed about each of them. When I complied, they would spend the balance of the class period with satisfied glows on their faces

For adults, work is usually the best antidepressant. Having a job makes us feel important, needed, and valued. The income we receive gives palpable evidence of our worth. But we still need our supervisors and colleagues to take notice of our contributions and mirror our joys and sorrows.

CHAPTER 6

NARCISSISTIC INJURY, REVENGE, AND RECOVERY

HOW DOES A CHILD recover from bullying or narcissistic injury by someone larger or stronger? We can all remember such moments: What we did was think of ways of getting even. Our vengeful fantasies soothed our rage and anguish. Where in reality we were helpless, in our imagination we regained control. Our musings also helped solve the problem of our isolation and loneliness by keeping whoever hurt us—usually a parent—mentally close at hand. This negative sort of intimacy was better than having no one there at all. We hoped that, if we showed how we were suffering, our tormentors would feel regret and make reparation. We also hoped that, next time, things would be different. Often we targeted our revenge on ourselves. As one adolescent commented after a suicide gesture, "How far do I have to go before my parents wake up?" In his mind, injuring himself was the only way to get his parents to take notice of his needs.

If the child's vengefulness is not dealt with constructively, it reappears later as part of their character, as their old grudges will find new targets. In my own therapy, there was a time when I realized that I had been projecting the source of all my woes onto my husband. My guilt and shame were intense, until my therapist made one of his unforgettable comments: "You need years of revenge to recover from your childhood." The sincerity in his voice convinced me of his empathy. His words strengthened and calmed me, and I was able to give up hating myself and eventually start accepting myself—such is the alchemy of therapy. Not having to wall off painful parts of my mind freed me to have new thoughts.

Eventually, I put my therapist to the test by speaking outright abusively to him. I said to him all the unforgivable things I wished I had been able to say to my mother. Some part of me needed to say them, to expel them out of my nervous system, despite another part of me that knew it was ridiculous, pure displacement. But hadn't he encouraged me to say everything? His surviving my words knit together the anguished parts of my soul. He proved that he'd really meant it when he told me to feel and say everything. I could venture into the darkest corners of my mind without fear of being exiled. It was okay.

Do we ever outgrow our taste for vengeance? Cultural evidence indicates otherwise. *Schadenfreude*, glee at another's misfortune, is ever ready to sate our appetite for retribution. So are the plot lines of fairy tales, much of literature, detective fiction, action movies, and the like. But ultimately, success is the best revenge, demonstrating to parents or other hurtful adults that, in effect, "I don't need you." But this is not altogether true. We do need them. Even as adults.

Here is Charlotte Bronte (1844) giving voice to ten-year-old Jane Eyre's feelings about her guardian who has just accused her of lying:

> *I am not deceitful: if I were, I should say I loved you, but I declare I do not love you: I dislike you the worst of anybody in the world. . . . I am glad*

*you are no relation of mine: I will never call you aunt again as long as I live.
I will never come to see you when I am grown up; and if any one asks me how
I liked you, and how you treated me, I will say the very thought of you makes
me sick, and that you treated me with miserable cruelty.*

Isn't this what each of us as children longed to say at one time or
another to an adult tormentor? Bronte's work was considered morally
corrupt in her day. Simply for being a little girl, Jane Eyre was expected
to respect her elders by properly suppressing her feelings. Indeed,
many children stifle their anger at their parents, fearful that not doing
so would lead to abandonment. Adults have all the power. And the
child wonders, *What if I had a bad wish and it came true? What if I told my parent
I hated him and then he actually died?* "Step on the crack/Break your mother's
back" is a childhood chant frequently heard in sidewalk play. To the
small child, not yet clear about the distinction between wish and reality,
the dread is that, not just words, but even thoughts can harm and kill,
and the child fears this potential of their mind.

I noticed my twenty-one-month old granddaughter did not like
it when I said, "Good-bye," at the end of a visit.

"No! No!" she whimpered, tears welling up.

"Go on—give Grammy a kiss good-bye," her mother urged.

"No!" She wouldn't. Was withholding the kiss a form of revenge?
Perhaps it was proto-revenge, an attempt to control my departure, not
yet the full-blown expression of an older child's sulk. I thought of a
solution: "Will you put a kiss in my hand so I can take it home to
Grampy?" That she was willing to do. I closed my fingers around it,
and as I turned to leave I noted that there were not the usual parting
tears. She had made a contribution without having to sacrifice her hurt
and anger about my leaving.

When a child is too overwhelmed even to fantasize, an emotional emergency occurs. Their only recourse is to collapse inward, blanking out their mind. They may look like they are coping, but inside nothing has been forgotten nor forgiven. They may target themselves in their need to punish, or their demon may lie in wait for the time when they are bigger and stronger, and can take it out on someone smaller or weaker. Meanwhile what little energy they have is diverted from a constructive path. They may use their very lives to communicate their need for revenge, and turn themselves into living testaments to their parents' failure by their refusal to grow up. The way most often chosen is failure at school.

Psychotherapy provides a way to work effectively with vengeful impulsivity. My interest is in how the process of working through a failure in a relationship can be very healing, creating a binding tie that continues to nourish well after the event. I will illustrate first with an anecdote about my then seven-year-old nephew, Alex, and then with some other anecdotes involving children and adults I have worked with over the years. Small children, who are by nature both passionate and candid, have a lot to teach about all kinds of emotions.

A. HELPING ALEX

I was visiting my family in Hawaii for several days on the occasion of my father's eighty-fifth birthday. Staying at his house halfway up the slopes of Haleakala, we composed a group of eight. In descending order by age, we were: my dad, my sister, me, my oldest younger brother, my youngest brother, his wife, and my oldest younger brother's son, seven-year-old Alex. There is a minimum age gap of fifty years between Alex and the rest of us.

Alex is a high-energy child who has had to endure the rancorous breakup of his parents' marriage. He soon gets bored and cranky and resorts to irritating us adults to manage his tension. On the occasions when we all get together, I am always torn between wanting to socialize with the adults and wanting to respond to Alex's needs. Usually my heart goes out to the little guy, and I make myself available to him. I have no competition from the balance of my family for this role. Instead, I am considered peculiar for my interest in children, though they are grateful for my keeping him out of their hair.

Seeing me after each separation, Alex asks, "Remember the time we played 'garbipils' on Christmas?"

"I certainly do," I reply.

He had been two and a half then, and when we played the toddler's favorite game of "chase me," he would squeal with horror and excitement, "Run! The 'garbipils' are coming!" I ferreted out that "garbipils" meant garbage men, toward whom he felt great awe and fear that year. Our race down the hall ended in my father's bedroom, where I would heave him onto the pile of pillows on the big bed. In our game he had become a bag of trash hurled into the maws of a giant, growling garbage truck. My role was both ally and monster as he worked on his dread in our vigorous play.

That year we started each morning by accompanying my dad on his daily hike up the lane behind his property—up, up, and up to its end, only a quarter of a mile in distance, but given an altitude change of four hundred feet, a challenging work out. On the second morning Alex had trouble with his socks, which kept sliding down into wads in the toes of his rubber boots. At first I responded to his plea, "Hey, wait for me," when he fell behind. But at some point I got caught up in conversation with my sister and sister-in-law about the elaborate meal we would be cooking for the birthday dinner that night. At some point

I realized Alex had fallen behind. I saw him down the hill a ways and read his body language—his downcast face, the hunch of his small shoulders, the way he was scuffing his boots at the side of the road. But I consciously made what felt like a selfish disconnect, a small, ordinary act of cruelty. Instead of mustering the patience to go down and join him, I turned back to enjoy the invigorating hike and chatter.

Alex never made it to the top of the lane, but no one commented on his absence. The rare car has to crawl in first gear, and Alex knows his way back. But on our return, as we reentered my father's property and each went our separate ways, I heard him call out to me from behind a little tree, "Now you know how I felt when you didn't wait for me." Hearing the timbre of hurt in his voice, I instantly understood. My abandoning him had hurt him, and so, by quitting the hike, he had abandoned me. He assumed I was feeling the same painful rejection he had felt.

His tone struck me to the quick. I had the urge to comfort him, to hold him, to make it up to him. I was so glad that I had my therapeutic skills to help him and help myself. I began by mirroring both his anger and his pain: "Oh, Alex, I'm so angry at myself. I did a terrible thing leaving you behind like that."

"Yeah. You knew my socks were falling down, and you didn't wait for me."

"You're right! I'm so sorry. It was unforgivable of me to do that!" We continued in this vein for a few exchanges, and then, arriving at the house, he invited me to play a game of Go Fish with him. He polished off his revenge—and his recovery—by creating his own rules (to which I did not object), ensuring that he would triumph over me, and we became cozily intimate once more.

Through this drama in which his accusation of neglect was accepted and then worked on with further talk and play, Alex's trust in me was restored. We were narcissistic twins once more. It is my hope that memories such as this become embedded in him as they do in me, a shared connection, part of the protective shield we each erect to tide us over our awful moments. In a way, I become "his" and he becomes "mine," like what the author of *Le Petit Prince,* Antoine de Saint-Exupery, has the fox say to the Little Prince about the rose with her four small thorns that he has cultivated on his minuscule planet: "It is the time you have wasted for your rose that makes your rose so important. . . . Men have forgotten this truth. . . . But you must not forget it. You become responsible, forever, for what you have tamed. You are responsible for your rose." Her thorns suggest her potential to hurt him, adding poignancy to the Prince's affection for her. The taming, Exupery implies, goes both ways. Similarly my taming Alex, who has many challenging "thorns," makes him mine and me his.

In the stiff-upper-lip culture of my family, feelings are swept aside as something to ignore and overcome. "Forget it. Just get on with your life." But they are unaware that there is a dual price to pay. When children are not helped to feel and manage difficult emotions and impulses such as rage and revenge, their destructiveness goes underground only to reemerge as self-defeating defenses. And there is another price: a loss of intimacy. With their feelings hidden, children are kept at a distance from others and from themselves, except for a persisting internal sense of conflict and pain.

B. GERRY, MY MOST CHALLENGING CASE

Compound despair in a young child with a parental model of violence and abandonment, and the result can be appalling. Gerry, aged twelve when he was brought to my office, behaved like a deranged toddler. This was not surprising, given that, following his parents' divorce when he was nine years old, his mother had placed him in a state facility for incorrigibles while she kept his older sister at home with her. When Gerry's father learned that he could take the boy out of the institution so long as he provided a home, he did so at great cost. Gerry had no more feelings for his father than he did for the small animals he would torture and kill. A child aged twelve with the feelings of rage, despair, nothing to lose, and no one to listen can inflict terrible damage. Ultimately Gerry was his own worst victim, but it could have gone otherwise. He was destructive in every way he could imagine.

I got some understanding some months later, when I first spoke with his mother after Gerry had landed in a hospital with serious injuries. She revealed psychotic denial and disconnection from her child by the one thing she wanted to impress on me: "My only concern is that Gerry not marry outside of our religion." A repeated suicide attempter herself, she believed Gerry required institutionalization in order to survive. Though she was briefly attentive while Gerry lay barely conscious and in great pain on a hospital bed, she retreated into unavailability once his physical condition improved. Heroically, his father persisted for years in his attempt to give Gerry a new start, with ultimate success.

In my office Gerry took revenge for his past traumas by frightening his father and me. He refused to attend school. He vandalized the homes his father rented. He stayed up all night, making noises, exhausting his father. He assaulted his father verbally and sometimes physically. Once, having grown to the size of a man, he began to punch his father in my office, so that I was forced to call the police. I always felt Gerry was on the verge of impulsively smashing something in my office, diving through my window, or bulldozing right over me in his rush to go out the door. Fortunately, my office at that time let out into my back yard, where Gerry could hurl apples fallen from my tree at squirrels, birds, and my garage.

Aside from telling him that certain behaviors were out of bounds, my main treatment intervention was a cheerful receptivity to seeing him and his father each week. Very gradually I helped Gerry develop the habit of talking, which at first was mostly to boast about his misdeeds. It took two years until the moment came when I thought to ask him a pivotal question: "Gerry, should I be afraid of you?" Looking startled, he objected, "No! I like you. I want to grow up and study to be a psychotherapist like you."

Gerry's desire to grow up and become a psychotherapist like me was evidence of our connection. As I have said a number of times, we grow in relationship to someone else. After declaring that he didn't want to scare me, he never did it again. Not long thereafter he started bringing an alcoholic twenty-year-old to his sessions, wanting to help this older boy as I had helped him. It was as if this man were his own first therapy patient. He also got a job sweeping up hair in a beauty salon. But due to circumstances in his father's life, we did not have time to work through this last phase of treatment together. He did call me once when he was eighteen to tell me he was now on friendly terms with his father's girlfriend, whom formerly he had tried to frighten and drive away. He, his father, and his father's girlfriend were living together, and his father's girlfriend was making delicious food for him. Having attached, Gerry became human.

c. Carla's Narcissistic Revenge

Sometimes patients play out narcissistic revenge by sounding as if they are about to abort treatment, the ultimate payback to a therapist.

Carla, for example, told me she had come to the conclusion that I had failed to rescue her from her life. Speaking one day in a soft, tense voice, she began a tirade that rose to a climax: "You know, for years I had been trying to please you. I believed that this would be my salvation, the way to turn around my lifelong depression. You knew my second husband was paranoid, but you let me marry him! All these years I tried to understand and help him, because I believed that was what you wanted me to do, instead of getting what I want. And there was the time he and I went away on a romantic weekend. I got all dressed up in my prettiest clothes and makeup. His only response was to accuse me of deliberately sitting against the wall in the restaurant facing outward so I could flirt with the maitre d'. How could you have let me marry that man?" Carla was revealing that she believed that I had the same thoughts as she did, and that I had known her second husband would be a disappointment and had failed to warn her. In truth, I had no way of knowing these secret thoughts that she had never told me.

In a self-righteous tone, she went on to tell me she was not angry with me. No, she was "disappointed." Almost as an aside she noted that she saved her angry shouts at me for the times when she was riding in her car on the way to or from her sessions with me. She faulted me further by saying that her recent gains in self-assurance and assertiveness had resulted solely from her own hard-won insight, distinctly not from anything I might have contributed. In short, I had been as big a failure to her as her parents had been. I refrained from saying a word until, at some point toward the end of the session, I commented, "I'm not going to point out that you're doing a good job this session."

As a writer, Carla knows how to choose words that wound. "Disappointed" conveys something deeper than anger, which can be just a flash in a pan. Also, her use of this word put her on a level with me, assuming the role of an authority sitting in judgment on me. I felt painful spasms of guilt and self-doubt. Perhaps I deserved to have her walk out on me forever? Yet as she gathered her things to leave, the abiding intimacy of our connection came out in her tone of voice as she chirped, "See ya next week!"

In an article titled "Hate in the Countertransference," a psychotherapist named Donald Winnicott writes about children's need to feel that they have an impact on those in their environment, but equally to feel that they are not omnipotent. They need their mother to survive their worst assaults and return to them in a cheerful humor. This reassuring cycle eventually enables them to recognize that they have hurt her and then to feel remorse about it, thereby recovering their sense of themselves as loving and lovable. In Winnicott's view, guilt is the antecedent of love. Similarly, patients need to test out and prove that the full expression of their anger affects but does not destroy the therapist. It is as if untested love is only a thin veneer of a real connection.

Vengeance is an ever-lurking potential of our mind. When we can't talk about it, it goes inward and embitters our heart. While resentful rumination is gratifying, it also creates a burden of guilt and pain. Only if we can speak it to someone who understands can we let the feeling be what it is meant to be—a flurry of emotional energy that, like a weather system, moves on as another one replaces it in the ongoing flow of life. The therapist's role is to loosen the stranglehold of buried resentment and enraging memory. It is also our role to bring our culture forward by getting the word out about this and other difficult feelings that our fears turn into our prisons. We need to normalize difficult emotions through talk and more talk, widening the space for children (and adults) to recover from their traumas, large and small. Our human need for narcissistic reassurance and love opens us to hurt and betrayal. Therapeutic treatment heals through applying wisdom and knowledge—and the therapist's own mended heart.

CHAPTER 7

LEARNING
TO BE POWERFUL

A. A LIVING NIGHTMARE

My TEACHING CAREER BEGAN as a nightmare. I was twenty-two years old, living alone in New York City. I expected my students to be shy, docile, and easily intimidated, as I had been at their age and for the most part still was. In my narcissism I couldn't conceive of their being different from me. I thought grades would matter, and that the threat of a phone call home would make them quake in their shoes. In short, I expected that they would tremble before me with the same terror as I had toward my teachers at their age. I also believed that, if I showed my interest in being their friend, they would wish to return my good will in kind. I could not have been more unprepared.

If I turned my back to write on the chalkboard, disturbances would break out. When I faced my students to teach my lesson on literature, vocabulary, spelling, or grammar, some of them looked everywhere except at me, as if I were of no importance to them. Their real interest seemed to be in teasing and provoking one another. I didn't want to yell and scream at them, but in my desperation and fear I did it anyway. I have a lot of amnesia about what went on that year. Fortunately, there were a couple of students who, despite my inadequacies, still wanted to please me, turning up each lunch period to wash my chalkboard and chitchat. Thank you, Henry and Carmen.

I was reluctant to do what some of my colleagues did, which was to assign busy work in the form of mindless worksheets or long lists of simple words to alphabetize and then look up in a dictionary. I really wanted to teach something, but I kept falling on my face. I stayed up late at night struggling with my lesson plans, worrying even as I slaved over them that they would fail. It was the most debilitating year of my life.

I was teaching five classes, two of which were "regular," meaning the students had reading levels close to grade level. The students in the other three could barely read. I was dumbfounded. These were seventh graders! They needed primers, not the thick, colorful textbooks available in the bookroom. But there were no primers. I was plagued with feelings of shame, shock, panic, stupidity, horror, and impotence. Somehow I plowed on. I tried reading to the nonreaders, for example the charming nonsense poem, "The Owl and the Pussycat," by Edward Lear:

The Owl and the Pussy-cat went to sea
In a beautiful pea green boat,
They took some honey, and plenty of money,
Wrapped up in a five-pound note.
The Owl looked up to the stars above,
And sang to a small guitar,
'O lovely Pussy! O Pussy my love,
What a beautiful Pussy you are,

You are,

You are!

What a beautiful Pussy you are!'

But when I got to the lines, "O lovely Pussy! O Pussy my love, What a beautiful Pussy you are," the children began to howl: "Teacher said 'pussy.' Teacher said a bad word!" They shrieked and guffawed and bawled it over and over and over— "Teacher said 'pussy!'" I was struck dumb. The glee with which they pounced on me! I had never seen anything like this in the suburban schools I attended. I had irresistible urges to lash out at them, and came close to doing so on one occasion.

When I gave my students a task to complete, I was lucky if twenty out of the thirty-five of them lifted a pencil. Meanwhile the others' papers ended up as missiles or in bits on the floor. I confess that I hated some of them. I was young and idealistic—and hateful? It did not square with who I wanted to be. I called in sick at least ten times in the course of that year.

In retrospect I can see that I expected that my being earnest and pleasant would get my students to like me and be nice to me. I had to come to terms with reality. They needed me to take charge, but for some reason I was paralyzed. Looking back I hypothesize my paralysis was the result of my never having had power in my entire life. I had been raised to be obedient, not powerful. I was afraid of the feeling of power!

B. I LEARN TO BE A RUTHLESS TYRANT

From my study of psychotherapy, I learned that I couldn't help my students (or later my patients) with any feelings that I couldn't tolerate in myself. My worst stumbling block was my aversion to feeling ruthlessly, tyrannically sadistic—the substrate of absolute power. I couldn't imagine wanting to do that, not even to my most hateful students. I had learned to bypass doing it by using the techniques I have written about above, but I confronted this lack head-on in my last ten years of teaching at the alternative school, when I decided to offer what I called "psychology classes."

What I had in mind was to teach psychology in a way that incorporated the principles of group therapy. Essentially, this is the way I always teach, but here the ante would be raised due to the powerful emotions that surface during spontaneous group process. My goal was to create "an arena for the emergence of difference," the same goal I consider ideal in a family. I would help members learn to be themselves as opposed to a clone of some model or ideal, because that is what promotes and restores emotional strength and resilience.

All well and good, except that I soon got the shock of my life—my first really dismaying experience in the classroom since way back in that initial year of teaching in the middle school. When, on the first day of teaching "psychology class," I asked my students my usual contract-establishing question, "What would you like to get out of studying this topic with me?" I got a startlingly different response from their usual "a passing grade." Instead, the outspoken ones (who generally are the spokespeople for a group) replied, "I want to learn how to read minds so I can use psychology on my enemies." Their goal was to increase their revenge skills! This was certainly not what I had had in mind!

But then I realized that their wish was simply diagnostic, informing me that they had been exposed to too much cruelty in their short lives, and in the backwash of my shock I felt compassion. Their stated goal revealed how fraught and dangerous their out-of-school lives were. I had to remind myself that it was not by chance that they had been thrown out of 2.5 schools before coming to that last-resort alternative school.

I gave them my instruction: "We are here to talk and learn to study the mind. We can talk about anything you like. How shall we begin?" The twenty-five seats in my classroom were arranged in a circle. Each group began in its own unique way. In one, a bold, verbal member might get the ball rolling by suggesting a question to answer in order to introduce themselves, or raising a hot topic, or in one case, the game of "killer" (in which one person by secret ballot becomes the killer and "kills" the others with a covert wink, whereupon each victim slumps in their chair until someone not yet dead is able to identify the killer). Another group might begin by avoiding functioning as a unit, instead forming subgroups, isolating themselves from one another by keeping their heads down or reading a book. Such groups excluded me altogether at first, resenting any of my attempts to get group communication going. Still others responded to my initial exploration by saying right off the bat that they wanted to talk about "sex and drugs and rock 'n roll." I knew to be patient and wait calmly for them to work up their courage to interact in whatever way they needed.

But almost at once I began to have doubts. I "got it" that their prevalent feelings were fear and distrust—of one another, of me, of spontaneous talking. But then, to my dismay, when they finally began to communicate, they did it by verbally attacking one another! When I tried to avert this line of interaction, I felt as though I were swimming upstream against a powerful current. It sent me running for help to the people who had trained me. That is how I learned that the problem was mine. I didn't want to feel my respondent sadism! I couldn't help them with theirs until I could embrace and manage my own. But how on earth was I to feel sadistic towards a population whom I saw as suffering and infantile? Essentially they were babies! Yet, feeling my way along, I gradually got into it. It was the key to my achieving eventual success.

With my tacit agreement, my students began to engage in sadistic teasing of one another in terms of clothes, appearance, behavior, sexual identity, family members, and so forth. They informed me that this is what went on in their favorite activity of "hanging out." They called it "snapping," or "the dozens." It was played directly with insults or indirectly with stealthy asides, withering glances, contemptuous tooth sucking, penetrating stares, or the like. It was a game, but it could easily escalate into a fight.

They informed me that this was often what went on in their families, too, where criticism and harsh physical punishment were the rule rather than the exception. One youngster reported that, in his home, he had to sleep with one eye open or his brothers would steal whatever he had or even strike him. I heard reports of violent abuse by stepparents, with the biological parent supporting the stranger over the child. Group members would bring in their babies or a relative's child and demonstrate their childcare techniques of terrorizing the infant with a belt, harsh commands, and shaming, oblivious to the distress of the baby. I felt anguished by seeing the tiny toddlers, dressed from head to toe like teenagers, dangling their tiny arms and hands limply at their sides, all liveliness squelched. When I drew the line at their abusing small children in my classroom, they once again accused me of being "white." They went on to say how they had seen white mothers permit their children to curse at them, which would never happen in their homes. Nonetheless, on this issue I was adamant.

I learned that they were accustomed to the game of snapping and knew its rules. Though some were more vulnerable, still they all had some practice at defending themselves. At last I put my courage to the sticking point and told them my new attitude: "Go ahead and kill each other off. I'll work with whoever's left." Shocking words to hear from the mouth of a teacher! Yet in time I succeeded in "out-bitching them," and by doing so I finally found a way to "mirror" them—to give them some needed narcissistic twinning. This got them to look at me with new respect. I assure you, however, that all my "snaps" were neutralized by my ordinary vigilant benevolence. I snapped in a goofy, exaggerated way, and exclusively to neutralize the most virulent "players."

For example, one angry girl announced that she had had a dream the night before in which I murdered all of her siblings. When I asked her what the dream meant, she replied, "I'm right to hate you. You killed everyone I love!"

I knew that dreams are wishes—in her dream she projected onto me her own desire to kill her siblings—so I embodied my comfort with her impulse by replying, "Those suckers deserved to die."

"You're disgusting," she snarled.

Some of my students persistently criticized me and expressed contempt of me for the way I worked, yet they would sign up for my class semester after semester, and my attendance was always nearly perfect. When I asked them what kept them coming back, they told me that, though I was completely wrong, they liked to observe me and feel superior to me. Their feeling free to say these things was a sign of my success. I was helping them convert from being primarily action prone to learning to use their words. When they saw that their aggressive comments did not damage or upset me, and that I remained as friendly as ever after they had said them, the feeling of ease and safety between us began to grow.

Class sessions became charged with feeling and drama. Comedians often became the stars of the show, though sometimes it was a class bully, male or female, or a stylish player who could report on the hippest nightlife or sport the grandest clothes, or someone with a particular talent or eccentricity. I found I could temper the stimulation level by upstaging or attacking the worst attackers (those who dish it out generally can take it). An important treatment goal for this population—to immunize them to the toxic power of words and feelings, particularly humiliation—could be addressed by my joining in the fray. I could model ego insulation by my breezy responses to what in their view were grave insults, and through lightening the mood, make difficult feelings tolerable. I especially thought about the benefit of their expressing so much aggression in words. What gets talked out has less pressure to be put in action. It provides a far healthier discharge for frustration than their usual spiteful, avoidant, and self-defeating behavior.

Not only absences, but lateness as well, was all but eliminated as youngsters vied with one another for choice seats. I learned to shepherd the aggression in various ways: through asides to group members: "Look out for Tina—her middle name is 'Vicious,' and she's got razor blades on both sides of her tongue," after Tina had sniggered about someone's "fake gold," or "high-water [too-short] sleeves." Muhammad, like many of the males, had a bottomless appetite for humiliating girls with cutting remarks about vaginal odor or belittling jokes. Once I got to know him, the moment he would start such a snap, I beat him to the draw by revealing his punch line and reminding the girls about his perpetual misogyny. "Get ready. Here comes some more 'I hate women' talk."

At first, when Muhammad snapped on me about my glass eye, my face lift, my wooden leg, my flat ass, my skirt made from window curtains, my wrinkled old private parts that no one would desire, his words and the manic laughter from the group magically transformed reality, and I would inwardly deflate with shame. Yet in time I developed immunity to such vitriol. I learned all their tricks of "playing it off" with a comic rejoinder, a snub such as exaggeratedly sucking my teeth, or a casual wave of my hand as if brushing away a cobweb. I would also intervene with an aside to the group that gave me a needed discharge: "It looks like Muhammad wants me to hate him today. What's up?" Muhammad frequently took a roll of money out of his pocket and riffled it, commenting, "This is all girls are interested in."

"Money can't buy love," I would retort, throwing my ego strength on the side of the girls. But I salted away the realization that Muhammad felt love could only be gotten by paying for it. It helped me to maintain the feeling mixture of sympathy and hatred and admiration that Muhammad, like so many of these youngsters, needed from me. Disarmed, he could be fun and funny, eager to impress with his stylish outfits and dramatic stories. As a group dominator, he provided a welcome diversion in the beginning weeks of one group's life. But eventually the more reserved members tired of his supremacy and found ways of getting heard and known themselves.

One day Muhammad came to class regally dressed in white from head to toe, except for a smudge of dirt on his backside. Group members immediately began to snap on his bowel incontinence. At first he wanted to go home and change clothes, but then he discovered that, by untucking his shirt, he could cover the embarrassing area. "Good save!" I complimented. The following day he sat next to a girl who was holding her baby on her lap. Theatrically pulling at the waistband of the infant's diaper, he quipped, "The bargain brand."

"Well, Muhammad, what brand were you wearing yesterday?" another student shot back, getting a huge laugh.

I sometimes detoxified the snapping by objectifying it: "That was memorable!" I might compliment, writing it down in my notebook, or "Tacky!" and wrinkle my nose. Members of the group with stronger egos began to teach the rest of us how to defuse the game with modest good humor. "You got me!" one shrugged mildly after being caught with mismatched socks in a game they called "tube check." (In this game, everyone would obligingly lift their pants' legs to reveal whether their socks' cuff stripes matched in color and number.) Group members loved it when I wrote down their best snaps and subsequently pulled out my list to use in another context. "How come you have to bite [copy] our lines?" some would gripe, but later they would plead for me to read from my lists:

"If I'm lying, I'm flying, and I ain't take off yet."

"What's so funny—you looking in the mirror?"

"You ain't got no sense—but I got dollars."

"W, x, y is you in my business?"

"This is an A and B conversation, so C your way out."

"Back off, hernia drip."

"So what—you want a dog biscuit?"

"You're funny as a funeral."

"Take a chill pill, keep still, and don't act ill."

"What movie was that in?"

"Stick your head in your ass and see how that fits."

Some snaps were comebacks: to "Shut up!" they'd reply, "Shut don't go up!" To "Kiss my ass," "Bend over and pucker up." (My own contribution! I loved saying it! It proved I could be even wilder than they.)

To any snap about appearance, "You ain't all that, either." To any snap about clothes, "Did you buy them?"

Some I originated. On being called a bitch, I would retort, "Damn straight. My ambition is to be the bitchiest bitch in the Western Hemisphere. No, make that the universe. Bitches live longer!" (This happens to be true, probably because nasty people dump their tension and aggression onto others.) Some were in Spanish: "*Bochinchera!*" an emotionally charged word meaning "malicious gossiper." "*Secreta reunion es mala educacion!*" meaning "a secret meeting [gossip] causes trouble." But a petite sixteen-year-old named Lucy (who was already a mother of two toddlers) trumped us all with her response one day. "You bitch!" one of her groupmates had snarled at her—apropos of what, I don't remember. "Now, wait a minute!" Lucy replied, her hand cocked on her hip. "I want some respect! Call me '*Miss* Bitch,' you hear?" We all howled.

Inner-city teens groom themselves with great care, thinking thereby to be impervious to snaps, but snaps did not have to make much sense to have a sting. Hilliard, true to the convention of the time, hit on anyone wearing more than one or two colors: "You look like you had a fight with a crayon box and you lost!"

"Listen to the monotone-wearing colorphobe," I once retorted, scoring a laugh.

Other times only I would laugh at some attempted comeback of mine, and they would try to get me down by saying, "How come you're the only one laughing?"

"At least someone's having fun," I'd reply, modeling my ego's comfort with the feeling of ostracism.

Everyone seemed to benefit. The stars from getting the limelight, the more timid ones from enjoying the show and indirectly learning so much about one-another's characters and aggression. But the miracle was that, over time, even the most virulent snapper revealed his pathos and became human. Group cohesion developed. The groups became deeply depressed and angry if I admitted a new member, and conversely mobbed me if I ever threw anyone out, which on one or two occasions I had to do. At length quiet ones would start talking, and new stars would emerge. My groups got the reputation for transforming formerly nice, shy youngsters into outspoken jokesters.

Whereas, in the beginning stages of the group, the members sat in guarded withdrawal, as they started to play together in the familiar manner of the street, they began to develop interest in each other. I thought about how wonderful this was. Connecting has the therapeutic effect of lessening their narcissistic self-absorption and isolation. I also saw that my own nonjudgmental and sustained interest in everything they had to say stimulated intimate interest in one another. Emotional arousal and discharge in the game of snapping led to the expression of other thoughts and feelings, though, like the oral aggression in snapping, much of their talk and impulsivity was from the oral stage of development (age birth to two).

All teens regress as they cope with the maturational task of separation and individuation, but these young people were at an extreme. Their grandiosity, their belief in magic, their focus on revenge, their extreme neediness, moodiness, psychosomatic difficulties (asthma, menstrual cramps, headaches, even ulcers), constant complaints of being tired and hungry, sexual fantasies and propositions towards me (which I understood as the desire to be back at the breast), and agitation at impending separations all communicated the infantile level of their emotional functioning. I realized that every one of them was starved for tenderness, interest, and care. How could my heart not go out to them?

My treatment plan focused on helping them talk spontaneously while I remained steadfastly there, day in and day out, calm and reassuring. I was the ready-for-play adult, giving them full, noncritical attention, as well as symbolic feeding through offering generous supplies of tissues, paper, pencils, and the like. Helping themselves to my tissue boxes was an indicator of their developing attachment to me, as was their request for other services, such as—on more than one occasion—when I sewed up a hole in a torn garment.

Although at first their communications were predominantly from the oral phase (age birth to two—mostly in the form of biting remarks), in time impulses from later developmental stages appeared. Anality (age two to four) was expressed in littering, writing graffiti, messiness and/or compulsive tidiness in their written assignments, anal words, stories about defecation and odors, jokes about anal sex, fascination with, and phobia about, homosexuality, and anal-stage theories about childbirth. I heard several times their belief that men could have "jelly babies that are weak and don't live very long."

After littering my room or in some other way being disrespectful, group members would tell me their surprise that I did not punish or scold them but instead persisted in encouraging them to talk, not act. I kept a broom in my closet to sweep up their leavings. "I'd rather you mess up my room than mess up your lives," I would say. "But how about putting your communication into words?" They were astonished that I did not mind being called a name or told "Fuck you."

"Would you let your own children at home talk that way to you?" they asked. "White people let their kids swear at them," they sneered.

But I would repeat, "Isn't it just a way of saying you're angry?" And I would tell them stories I had heard from other students about how they would never speak crossly to their mothers, but when they were doing the dishes, they might deliberately break a treasured heirloom platter. "But how do you teach your children respect?" they asked.

"The same way I teach you—by showing it."

"Oh," one observed. "That's hard work."

There were one or two occasions when a child overtaxed my tolerance, and I would arrange for him or her to take time out or switch to another class. After I told a girl named Estelle of my plan to transfer her, she protested, "Why? I just do what everyone else does." Estelle had no awareness of the degree of irritation she caused me.

"I don't understand it myself," I said (and I didn't!), "but I'm fed up with you."

"You mean I have to analyze you?" she whined.

"Might be a good idea," I replied. I let her come one final time, and to my amazement she was fine. I never found her intolerable again.

Expression of phallic (age four to five) impulsivity emerged: competitiveness, boasting, stories about sexual prowess, masturbation, gun notching, and sexual anxieties. The boys would bring up worries about inadequate penile size. "Every size is perfect," I would reassure them. Kit, a big strong girl, once came up to me after a class in which the boys had outdone themselves with their phallic braggadocio. Whispering in my ear she told me as she nodded towards her genital area, "You know, I am really well cut!"

"Teacher is a sex maniac," students would snap as I tolerated all this posturing.

But I would just give a little dismissive wave of my hand and tell them, "You are free to think whatever you wish." The boys shared their concerns about potency and the embarrassment they suffered when they ejaculated too quickly or when girls saw their facial contortions at the moment of climax. The girls, sexually active but worried about their reputations, wistfully mourned their virginity as the boys jumped in with jokes about women whose vaginas had stretched to the size of the Holland Tunnel. "Nonsense," I would say, and teach them about perineal exercises that tighten and firm.

Their requests for sex information revealed their fears and primitive conceptual level:

"Can a penis get so hard it'll bleed?"

"Is earwax an effective contraceptive?"

"Can a girl get pregnant by swallowing sperm?"

"Can a dog get a woman pregnant?"

Their general horror in regard to oral sex revealed their underlying confusion about anatomy and the separation of elimination products from sexual ones. The boys would share their seduction secrets with one another. Aware of the girls' need to absolve themselves of responsibility, they recommended, "Never ask a girl for sex, because she'll just say 'no.' What you gotta do is just silently keep on making your moves." This seduction method ruled out barrier birth control, which was too deliberate, too adult. Withdrawal prior to ejaculation was the only method of birth control I heard them willing to use with any consistency. Guilt also played a role because they believed that, if a girl was willing to spread her legs, she should be willing to have the baby. In an aside to me, one sixteen-year-old boy confided that, when he was fourteen, he had had his sperm checked because he had never gotten a girl pregnant. I learned further that some of their fathers had many "wives," and that it was a prideful thing to have a bevy of women attend one's funeral, all claiming to have been the one and only.

Drugs were a favorite topic, fitting so well into their adolescent regression. For the oral stage, drugs were "magic" mood alterers; for the anal stage, drugs were defiance and power. But I lay down my own cardinal rule about drugs, which had a covert, therapeutic punch: "I want you to come to class sober because I want to get to know you as you really are, not chemically altered." My message linked up with the healthy narcissism in their egos—I wanted the real them, not some drug-altered facsimile. Of course, a few would test me by coming in high. If I became aware of it, I used a technique of lending them my ego to help them give me appropriate behavior. That is, I would give soberants: Vitamin C from the bottle of chewable tabs that I kept handy for marijuana intoxication, milk for PCP, honey for alcohol, time out for cocaine.

Once I formed a group expressly for youngsters with a history of drug overdose. I began the group with an intervention playing on their adolescent negative suggestibility: "Everyone knows the dangers of drug use," I said, "so let's leave that boring stuff out." After some days of intense sharing, they tired of the subject and began to disclaim being "burn-outs." It was the last time I heard any of them boast about drug use. (This was the group who had all agreed that taking drugs was a way of hurting their parents in revenge for their own suffering.)

Jail was often discussed. Some were not afraid of the prospect, having been there or had friends or relatives who were incarcerated. When I heard stories of how some of their mothers managed to raise bail, I would marvel. Many of the girls found the idea of jail romantic and wished to have a pen pal who was incarcerated. Vivien reported how her boyfriend stole something for her, and how moved she was that he took this risk for her. "What if he got locked up?" I asked.

"Oh, there are plenty of other guys around," she said, smiling sweetly as she exposed her true colors.

"Another female with a vendetta against men!" I informed the group. Many of my interventions aimed at helping them learn to spot such malice in themselves and one another. I also warned them," I don't make jail visits!" to bring their criminal impulsivity into the relationship with me, since that was the true basis of my influence on their emotional growth. My covert message was that I wanted them safe, constructive, and present on a daily basis.

A parole officer wanted to bring a boy named Kent to me, but first for an entire semester I met weekly with his father, Dan. Dan was at his wit's end with his adopted son, who was doing graffiti and drugs and crimes of every sort. I worked to help Dan establish more realistic ways to understand and communicate with Kent, and then finally one day Kent himself showed up. Small for his age, Kent manifested his toughness by the heavy chains he wore around his waist, the clumpy boots that he left untied, and a coiffure that consisted of a sheet of straight hair through which only the tip of his nose protruded.

After several months of regular attendance, Kent appeared one day with his hair cut and styled so that, for the first time, we saw his handsome face. It was as if he had been reborn, and the girls began to pay some attention. Thereafter, Kent began to seem like just one of the crowd—until the last day of that semester, when he came in with a flask of whiskey concealed in a velvet pouch. When I spotted what he was up to, I told him he would have to put it away. We then had an exchange that escalated in tone from ordinary conversational to louder and louder braying, two donkeys really going at it:

Kent: "You're being ridiculous! This is the last day of school. Why can't we celebrate?"

Me: "I'm not going for it! You're trying to get me into trouble."

Kent: "No, I'm not. No one has to know! What's wrong with you?

Why are you so paranoid?"

Me: "Yeah? You want my license lifted! And my pension taken away. No! I'm not going for it. I didn't work all these years to have those things taken away!"

Kent: "Why are you carrying on? We have a right to have some fun on the last day of class."

Me: "No way! Out of the question! Go start your summer vacation early! Go! Celebrate all summer! I don't want to see you until September."

Kent was one of the first students to return to school at summer's end.

I found that, after a while in my groups, we all began to sound like one another, quoting one another, inviting one another's unique responses and points of view, missing one another if an absence occurred, picking up on one another's vocabulary, tastes, interests, ideas, and feelings. As group bonding increased, the students learned a new form of intimacy based, not on sadism, but on the deeper satisfaction of talking together openly and meaningfully. Did it work miracles? The main evidence I had of success was their increased intimacy together (no small achievement!), their almost perfect attendance, and their improved ability to relate to other teachers. I did not have the time or resources to do more rigorous research than this.

What I can speak about directly is the miracle that took place inside *me*. Not only did I learn to enjoy my sadism, I also developed immunity to any insult or criticism that could ever be thrown my way. All I have to do is think in my head, *I want some respect, you hear? Call me "Miss" Jerk (Idiot, Fool, Heathen, Whatever)!* and I start chuckling with fond remembrance. My students helped me make friends with my sadism, and I am the stronger for it.

C. SPEAKING THE UNSPEAKABLE

I spoke above of learning to love my sadism, but I think it is equally important to get comfortable with other emotions that are considered too shameful to mention. In human history, culture has all too often put a gag on what is natural to our biology, and the result is that we feel bizarre for having our darker feelings, sure that we are the only ones to do so. Keeping a vow of silence also forestalls our having a lot of fun. Let me reveal my own fantasy life: senior citizen though I am, as I walk down the street, in my mind I undress a lot of men and some of the women, too. I have lovely sexual fantasies. I also kill some people—an instant demise for those who menace me, sometimes just for being younger and lovelier or seeming better off in some way. I have daydreamed fatal lung cancer for my grouchy neighbor over the back fence. More torturously, I have imagined the death of each of my loved ones. I think I do this in part to prepare myself for the fact that the worst may happen to any of them at any moment. But as a therapist I know that such fantasies are wishes in part, too. By nature I am a beast, at least potentially. Under the right circumstances, I, too, could kill. I, too, could torture. I, too, am human.

What makes it so hard to acknowledge these feelings is that some part of our minds thinks simply having the thought or wish can make it come true, the residue of our childhood fantasies and dreams. Even into adulthood I caught myself reciting under my breath the child's rhyme, "Step on the crack/ break your mother's back," as I carefully avoided the lines in the sidewalk. My adult self knows that, if a wish could kill, no one on this planet would survive. Still, it was not that long ago that I was still watching where I placed my feet. I also notice how often I no sooner have a "forbidden" thought, than in some way or other I manage to hurt myself. I recall once when I had on a new suit; at the moment that I was thinking how fine I must look in it, I caught my toe in a sidewalk crack and fell smack down on my knees, bloodying them and tearing my stockings. Crime and punishment in a flash—even though it was only a "thought" crime! Why in my mind was it a felony to feel pride? Putting on my therapist cap, I find the answer in my old, hard-core feelings about my mother: She had made it clear that I was not to outshine her. She was the pretty one, and I was the awkward, pimply, stoop-shouldered nebbish. She could not tolerate me as a competitor, and there is still some part of her living on inside me that I need to protect (as well as protect myself from). Why don't I stop having such feelings? The answer is simple: When it comes to emotions, it is impossible to just "get over it." Emotional memories skulk in our subcortical brain, the part also called the "reptilian" brain. A reptile cannot obey the command, "Just snap out of it," and neither can I.

As a child I lived in fear and shame of my destructive feelings and fantasies. Since no one I knew ever voiced such things, I assumed I was the only one harboring them. I took it as further evidence that something was uniquely wrong with me. What we cannot talk about becomes unspeakable, as though to give it voice could unleash some horrendous genie of evil. But try as I might to have only the sweet, kindly thoughts I was taught were proper, others snuck in, especially after I had been criticized or frustrated.

When I lived down south as a teenager, my friends would often say on parting, "Be sweet," instead of "'Bye." I always felt congested afterwards, as if I needed to vomit emotionally. I hardly ever felt sweet inside. One outlet for my aggression as a child was to fantasize my own death, which for some years I would be sure to do when visiting my father. I relaxed in bed picturing the scene of my funeral, everyone lowering their heads as at last they realized how hurt I had been. Why did I have that fantasy at his house and not at my mother's? Perhaps because I knew he would really be sad, whereas I was never sure but that my mother might just be annoyed as usual. But also, the fact was he had not saved his marriage to my mother, so why shouldn't I want to punish that sweet man whom I also adored above all others?

Other than my fellow therapists and certain writers (and of course my patients and students, with my encouragement), I don't know anyone who engages in the free and open discussion of *Schadenfreude* or other cruel or scatological thoughts. Though many people enjoy violent movies and books, a sublimated form of such feelings and impulses, no one publicly acknowledges having them. Even when I hear people say, as they commonly do, "I feel like killing him," or "I'm gonna kill myself," I recognize it as just a figure of speech. No real feeling there. What a burden pretending to be innocent is.

Organized religion has often taught that aggressive and murderous thoughts and feelings were evil: "The sin begins with the thought." (Except for Buddhism, which for thousands of years has reassuringly portrayed all thoughts as simply passing clouds.) Fortunately, today many divinity schools no longer teach that thoughts can be sins, as some colleagues who are ordained clergy have informed me. Since a lot of their training is devoted to preparing them for their roles as pastoral counselors, they know that mental health depends on understanding and accepting even the worst human feelings and impulses (but not actions, just to reemphasize a point).

For the first forty or so years of my life I suffered from a lot of depression. I spent a great deal of time brooding in my marriage, for example, alternately blaming my husband and ferociously blaming myself for my misery. Luckily my husband, an artist, was too busy in his studio to notice much of what was happening in me. Thank goodness. I felt awful about myself in all the ways that it is possible to feel: "less than" in looks, achievement, possessions, intelligence, courage, ability to speak up, talent, taste, power, you name it. I had great difficulty asking for things for myself, even from vendors who took my money. Some memory response deep inside warned that any assertiveness on my part would create a threat to my survival. I had grown up apologizing for my very existence, and this continued well into my psychotherapy when I learned to be comfortable with feeling angry, the counterbalance to depression. Old emotional habits are impossible to jettison, for all that they are self-imposed.

D. A Cure for Depression

It is impossible to feel depressed and angry at the same time. That is why anger is so valuable—not acting angry, but feeling angry. (I do not recommend inflicting anger on anyone except after the utmost, conscious deliberation during which one's long-range as well as short-range goals are given thorough consideration). Now, as I gradually help my depressed patients feel anger, I rejoice as I watch them start to come alive. Most depressives are far too nice, as I once tried to be, except when it comes to themselves. My treatment plan is to turn them into emotional monsters, if only in their minds. One of my most recent depressed patients, Cassie, was slated for shock therapy before falling into my clutches. It took me the better part of two years of weekly sessions to help her start feeling comfortable with her rage.

Cassie grew up in a culture that demands women to be subservient to their spouses. She needed to learn how to feel powerful with her husband, and her husband needed to learn that to have a happy wife (versus a compliant, depressed wife); he had to stop expecting her to obey him all the time. All through their marriage he would berate her for any slips in her fulfilling her "responsibilities," meaning taking care of children, elders, and housework. But now, his scolding triggers passionate anger in Cassie, positively levitating her out of her chair. Fortunately, anger is not only healing, it is also fun, once it is accepted in all its intense though in reality impotent absurdity. Cassie will never convince her husband to think the way she does, but she has to give herself the right to feel angry and selfish and powerful anyway. Having these feelings will actually help her be a good wife and mother, because she will get her energy back. Depression is exhausting!

My job is to help Cassie and her husband express their feelings and respond to one another's feelings appropriately. All each has to do is listen to the other's grievances and say something like, "I hear what you are saying," and leave it at that to restore the other's sense of well-being. If they insist on explaining their feelings, they have to know that the other won't be able to take in a word they're saying. But Cassie's husband has noticed how animated she is when she gets enraged at him. He in turn gets cute by teasing me about paying his bill, and I threaten to hit him with my baseball bat. (I don't own one.) They exit, rolling their eyes, but laughing.

Larry, a new patient, can't stop blaming himself for everything that goes wrong in his life. He and I agree that his psychotic ex-wife, who stonewalls his wanting to see his kids, is poisoning their minds against him. Yet he still feels at fault. Then I hear about how his father, with whom he is living, takes every opportunity to fault him—for his thoughts, his habits, his weight, his less-than-prestigious job, for his not forcing his way back into his children's lives. His father's "helpful suggestions" are really emotional attacks in disguise. Larry loves his father, who is in many ways a kind, honest, and generous man, and he feels grateful to be able to live in his house temporarily. Therefore, he cannot fathom being furious at him—until I grab hold of his ear. (So to speak. I do not make physical contact with my patients). I ask him, "Is it okay that I feel enraged at your father for being so abusive?"

"You mean I'm not the only one who sees that in my father?" Larry responds, sounding relieved.

I then ask a question that really intends to teach: "Is it okay to have more than one feeling at a time, like both anger and gratitude towards your father?" I find most people are not aware that this is normal. Larry leaves my office with some bounce back in his stride.

E. Cussing Always Cheers Me Up

Forbidden language is perfect for those moments when I really need to get something off my chest. No other words vent the depth of rage and the joy of antisocial impulsivity as fully and safely. "Civilization began with the first man who hurled a curse instead of a sword," observed some ancient pundit. On second thought, sometimes the use of a wild hyperbole works as well as cussing, because the first example that came to mind was a conversation I had with Diane, a gym buddy, this week. Diane was complaining to me about how her mother cannot tolerate it if she does anything for her mother-in-law. "You took her to *that* tea house?" her mother says, at once welling with tears. "That's where *I* always wanted to go." "You gave her chocolates? What kind? You never gave me those!" Her mother cries for hours about these "slights," regardless of what Diane says to defend herself.

So Diane asks me what to do. I instruct her, "Tell your mother you've been a bad daughter."

"Yeah," says Diane, "she wants me to admit I do her wrong."

"So tell her! Tell her you are the worst daughter in the country—

no, in the whole universe!"

Diane starts laughing, but she still doesn't know I am serious. "Yeah, I told my mother I do more for her than I do for my mother-in-law, and I made a list to prove it."

"Reality is beside the point! You'll never convince her. Just tell her you're really a horrible, disgusting daughter in every imaginable way." Then I reminded Diane about what she had told me about her mother's history of having been abandoned in foster care when she was four. Her mother is a big baby who cannot stand sharing her "mommy" (whom Diane symbolizes) with another. So the fact that Diane will not give her mother one hundred percent of her time, energy, and resources means she is an awful daughter. But when it is said with overstatement rather than defensiveness, the other can get the point and laugh, too.

I love the cultural differences evident when it comes to cussing. "What does it mean when American kids say, 'Futch you or mother futcher?" a recently immigrated Chinese teenager asked me. After I explained, he still looked puzzled. "But why they say that?"

"Well, what do you say to someone when you are really angry at him?" I asked.

Lowering his face in shame, he mumbled, "I tell him I hope someone in his family gets sick. Then we have to fight!"

When my father was a teenager riding to high school on horseback in Lihue, Kauai, he got the nickname "Bayao," which in Tagalog means brother-in-law. But in his hometown milieu with its many Philippine sugar cane workers, "Bayao" had become an insult, meaning "cuckold." "You brother-in law, you!" This is not the style of cuss one hears in our culture.

Growing up with Japanese friends, I learned some really shocking insults that don't raise a hair when translated into English. "*Dae jobu*," for one. It translates as "You smell like a toilet." We don't usually get so metaphorical in English. Then there is "*Tashi bobo*," which, when I say it experimentally to Taki, my Japanese car repairman, makes him give a little jump. "You're a bad girl!" he shouts. (It translates as "Fornicate standing up like an animal.") Finally, there is one really terrible Japanese insult that my brother has been trying to teach me. It goes something like, "*Baka kava, shin dayo, anatano okasan debuso.*" He tells me its translation: "You eat like a hippopotamus, and your mother's navel protrudes."

But when I say this one to Taki, he scratches his head and shrugs. "Something about my mother being dead?" How can I not giggle when there is so much potential for mispronunciation as well as difference in intentional nastiness from one culture to another?

My husband, whose first language was Yiddish, has been teaching me words and phrases from the earliest days of our courtship, including curses. It wasn't long before I learned a delightful thing when we had a fight. If I cursed in English, "Go to hell!," he shrugged it off like a horse swatting a fly with a careless flick of its tail. But if I used Yiddish, "*Gae en dreart!*" he would turn red and glare at me. Oh, the power and the fun.

f. A Toddler's Curse

The youngest child I have ever worked with was two-and-a-half year-old Ellie. Her pediatrician referred her to me because of her "failure to thrive." She had stopped playing, eating, and sleeping. The only thing she wanted to do was suck aggressively on her pacifier, day and night. Despite her tiny size, her body seemed to give off sparks of stubborn determination as she toddled into my office behind her mother, pacifier firmly clenched in her mouth. In a brief background explanation, Ellie's mother informed me that Ellie's condition had started after she asked her to give up her pacifier because she "had to be a big girl now."

Oops. Not a good thing to say to a toddler, especially since Ellie's mother really meant it. My first task was to convince the mother to back off from pressuring her daughter while I had a chance to study and work with the child.

Our relationship began with Ellie ignoring my presence as she lay on her mother's bosom on the couch next to my chair. Ellie was squirming like a larva and picking at her mother's buttons. There was quite a long moment while she ignored my presence. Then she gave one swift peek at my eyes before glancing away. I gave a swift peek back. This gradually advanced to Ellie devising her own variation of peek-a-boo, with me following her lead, something like playing hide and seek with our hands over our eyes. When she needed to retreat, Ellie would bury her face in her mother's chest, and I would bury my face against the back of my chair. It got to be fun, with Ellie creating little surprises. Her mother asked me what I was doing, but I just pled for patience. I wasn't sure where we were going myself, but I trusted Ellie's need to engage me at her own pace and in her own way.

In later sessions our play progressed to an actual game of hide-and-seek, a challenge in the confines of my small office. Ellie or I would hide—behind a chair, under a jacket, under the blanket I kept at the foot of the couch, behind another chair, behind the chalkboard that leaned against the wall, our extremities poking out from the hiding spot but our faces well concealed. We took turns being "it." The one who was "it" hid, as the other counted to ten with her eyes closed, then began her search, pretending at first not to see, and then squealing loudly as she found the "it." There would be more giggles and shrieks and then we'd start all over again. I surmised that the urgency of the hide-and-seek game reflected Ellie's feeling of having been lost and wanting to be found.

I began to leave my file drawer open, so Ellie could discover my toy collection. At some point she found the puppet family: mother, father, older sister, older brother, and baby. With the puppet family Ellie continued to tell me the story of her life through her play. First, mother puppet was pregnant. (In reality, Ellie's mother *was* pregnant, and there was also a baby back at the house.) Ellie would stuff the puppet baby under mother puppet's dress. Sometimes she stuffed another family member under there, and once the whole family (including the father) until the mother puppet's dress was stretched to the point of bursting. Next, mother puppet was taken to the hospital so the doctor could take the baby out. A shoebox served as the ambulance, siren screaming as it raced mother puppet to the hospital next to my couch. Then Ellie would switch roles from ambulance driver to doctor as the shoebox converted to a hospital bed. At last the climax: Ellie would crush the mother puppet's belly with the heel of her hand, grunting with effort, and brutally flattening the shoebox with her pressure. Finally she tugged open the mother puppet's dress and yanked out the baby (and whoever else she had thrust in there). Was it a delivery or an assassination? This scene was replayed many, many times, with the high point always arriving when the doctor vigorously attacked the belly of the inert mother. Later, the game somehow morphed into the older-brother puppet pounding its hard rubber head against the mother puppet's hard rubber head, chipping small flecks of paint off in the process.

In subsequent months Ellie devised a game of "school" whereby she was the teacher and I was the obedient student. She taught me to do a proper somersault. She taught me a song she had learned at school. She taught me to write my ABCs (I was to copy hers exactly.) She had me duplicate the drawing she was doing on her drawing pad, handing me the correct color crayons to match hers and monitoring my efforts with an eagle eye. It was serious business. Meanwhile, I heard from Ellie's mother that Ellie was eating well, sleeping well, doing well at preschool, and had lost all interest in her pacifier.

One day, after about a year and a half of our working together, Ellie paused upon entering my office, looked up at me, and suddenly began to shout like a Nazi: "You are nothing! You are a window! You are a door! You aren't even there! You can't come to California with us!" Her voice rang out like a firecracker in a tin box. I stood there in shock and awe as this tiny, fierce person let me have it. She said the worst sentences that could possibly be said to a child, cussing me to a turn without using a single dirty word. And then I understood: She needed me to feel what she had felt when her mother urged her to grow up fast— like someone unknown, like someone who wasn't even there, like someone who would be abandoned by the family when they left for a dream vacation. Immediately following her outburst, our usual vigorous play resumed, as if she had never shouted those devastating things at me. It goes without saying that I was pleasant and coopera-tive with her as usual, demonstrating to her that I, too, could survive those awful feelings.

What went on in little Ellie's head and heart to bring her back to a state of vibrant health? Very much in the narcissistic stage of devel-opment (age birth to three years), she was telling me about herself in the only way she could—by getting me to feel what she had felt. At her age she had not the words, thoughts, or perspective to say what was troubling her. She could only do what a child does—enact her trauma through play. My practice as a therapist is to make myself available to anyone with whom I work. People of all ages assume I have the same thoughts and feelings as they do, and I never disabuse them of this notion. (Actually, no thought or feeling is foreign to me, so in some sense it is true.) I know that my being their emotional echo strengthens their egos, fortifying them to face reality better, bit by bit, as they become ready to do so.

As a first-born child, Ellie, rather than recognizing herself as the small child she was, identified with the adults in her world. She wanted even more than most children to please her mother and do as her mother wished. However, her mother's request that she "be a big girl now" had been too much for her, and so she had collapsed inward with her "failure to thrive," a sort of symbolic death. She needed help recovering her spontaneity and optimism, as well as to express her frustration at having been pressured to grow up according to a timetable that was not her own. This is how I understood her drama as it culminated in her marvelous outburst of cussing me on that momentous morning. By then Ellie's recovery of strength, and good feelings about herself—the two go together—was becoming evident.

Ellie's mother, a highly educated professional, was always present in Ellie's sessions with me. In the beginning she was puzzled, asking me to explain what I was doing. Later I noticed her imitating the way I worked with Ellie, helping Ellie live out her fantasies, as children need to do. She began to understand my operational plan. Children work on their feelings through play. Ellie's mother eventually referred other family members to me, indicating her respect for my work. I, in turn, feel fortunate and grateful to have learned so much from them.

CHAPTER 8

APPLYING WHAT
I HAVE LEARNED

A. A THERAPIST'S JOB IS TO SURVIVE
THE WORST FEELINGS

"I CAN'T LISTEN TO what they say," the teacher said. "They're too sad, too upsetting. I feel so helpless." He was a member of my training group for high school teachers on how to listen to inner city adolescents, but he was finding out that hearing their tragedies was more than he could bear. He quit my group and undoubtedly went back to entertaining his students. He was a talented performer, and perhaps that was his best way of connecting with them.

True, it is difficult to listen to some people talk about their lives. The stress of it is endemic to my trade. My mentors constantly remind *me* to take vacations and give *my* brain a rest. But I will tell you this: No television show, no Broadway play, no novel, and no film could be more fascinating and intense than the stories I hear as a therapist. Still, the question of why it is so hard just to listen is an interesting one. I ask myself if I truly enjoy doing it. I answer, "Most of the time." Then what is so difficult to hear and feel? And why do I do it? Early on in my training, I struggled with the idea that, if I heard about a problem, my job was to find some way to fix it, as the teacher cited above seemed to feel. I didn't have the long-term perspective to know that internal change takes place at a glacial pace (pre-global warming, that is). I also didn't know that people's problems are part of their personal way of dealing with life, so no matter how torturous their particular system, it is better than having no strategy at all, for that could mean psychosis. Now, with forty years of experience, I have no problem just listening without trying to make changes. I don't have to figure out solutions for my patients. Change comes just from talking fully and freely about one's life.

It is particularly hard to be with a complainer like my patient Jim. Listening to his tone of voice is like having heartburn, achy and endless. His talk is an infant's distress cry, compelling and unbearable at the same time. It gets me to want to go into action when there is no action that could be taken. Sometimes I want to scream, "Stop it!" Instead I ask, "So what choices do you have?" or give him the order, "You've said that already. Say something new!"

For many years Jim's pattern was to pursue glamorous women who would first exploit and then reject him. Time went by, and he still seemed to be complaining about the same thing. And then one day he surprised me by making a forward leap: He got a challenging new position in his industry. Then, within a year, he became engaged to a mature, nurturing woman, and together they bought their own home. Of course, now it is his wife who takes the brunt of hearing the whine in his tone of voice. Jim knows better than to use it, but as he says, "It's so much more satisfying when I complain than when I just say what I want."

I think whining gives him an internal massage. Also, I think there is an unconscious fantasy of punishing his mother. Anyway, now that he is able to observe himself and talk openly about it, I know he can choose not to do it. As Freud once said about someone emerging from a neurosis, in place of seeking perfection he can "settle for ordinary misery." His relinquishing his magic hope—for pure love, pure solace for his miserable childhood, pure understanding—has enabled him to live with the minor disasters (mostly involving people disappointing him) that erupt in his daily life.

Years ago, my inner city high school students would sometimes come into my classroom when I was alone, wanting to talk. Usually it was to disclose something that was frightening them, and on a few occasions the subject was a murder the teen claimed to have committed or witnessed. One boy told me he had murdered three guys who had been harassing his girlfriend. Was it the truth? He certainly seemed agitated as he described what happened. In that instance I spoke to my principal, and he called the boy's alcoholic mother, who denied that anything had happened. According to the rules of confidentiality, I am forbidden to reveal what goes on in a consultation with me unless I have the idea someone is either going to hurt themselves or someone else, but the incidents I heard about were always after the fact. It was not my job to be a police mole, yet listening to such stories was haunting, and furthermore, after telling them to me, the young people sometimes disappeared, leaving me with clouded thoughts about what had become of them.

And how naive some of my inner-city students could be! One wrote me a letter after he disappeared, explaining that he had been put in jail for a "Mister Meaner" and asking for help. The thing I most remember about this particular boy was the way he frequently made strange animal-like sounds in the classroom. None of us teachers could make sense of this until, one day, someone spoke by phone with his father and heard the identical grunts and honks. Was the father recreating his original agrarian environment in this way?

My private patients are basically middle-class, high-functioning citizens, but their stories can still be very upsetting. Listening to them, I live their distressing lives alongside them. Most extreme has been a family I have been seeing for ten years, the Ls. I soon learned that the two most impossible members of the L. family were the mother and the first-born son, Tony, though that is not what they originally presented to me. Back then it was the middle son, Ben, and his irritable bowel syndrome that got them to seek help. Perhaps bringing Ben was a way to test me. Ben's body healed right up, whereupon Tony became the focus of the family's anxiety, and soon thereafter, emerging from the background, his mother, Catherine, as well. Not long after I started to work with them, the father called to tell me that Catherine was attacking Tony with a pair of scissors.

"Violence in the home is illegal!" I exclaimed. "The police must be called." When they showed up, Catherine claimed that Tony had attacked her. The police took her to a hospital anyway, but she was released almost immediately. When she wanted to, she could make herself appear normal. In the subsequent years I continued hearing the often-horrifying saga of the L. family. It was always either Catherine or Tony having protracted tantrums, destroying things around the house, tormenting the long-suffering father, getting drunk, and so forth. But there were no further incidents of personal violence until recently, when Catherine, having reached menopause, began physically attacking her husband. Catherine, as I discovered, is on the far end of the borderline schizophrenic spectrum. She blames her abusive behavior on whomever she is abusing, which now is usually her husband.

But when she begins a sentence on any topic, she will change theme several times before she comes to the period at the end of the sentence, regressing with each shift. She has had only two or three brief hospitalizations and generally refuses to take medication, but she can be delusional, especially with her husband.

The L. family member I want to concentrate on here is Tony, who had to survive child abuse by his mother from the day he was born. Catherine told me she had intentionally neglected him as a way to get back at her husband. Later, for the same reason, she physically abused him with kicks and punches when he was a toddler. By the time he was fifteen, Tony got into drugs, and the family threw him out. A handsome young man with bright green eyes and a six-hundred-watt smile, Tony attracts the girls (young girls love damaged boys!). He got into his first serious trouble at the age of eighteen, when a fifteen-year-old girl's mother pressed charges against him for statutory rape. At the girl's request, Tony had necked with her, going so far as to touch her vagina with his finger, also at her request. That was the extent of his sexual molestation. While Tony was being arraigned, the fifteen-year-old was in a motel with a thirty-five-year-old man, but that didn't stop the wheels of justice from snaring Tony in their relentless spin. He naively signed a statement proffered by the police in return for being released, and then was made to serve some months in jail before being put on parole for life under Megan's Law. This means he has to attend a weekly sex offender's group (basically a maturational experience for him, even though he doesn't belong there!) and to be repeatedly humiliated and harassed by his town's police department, the standard procedure with Megan's Law offenders.

In Tony's initial sessions with me, I could not tell whether he was psychotic. He told me about engaging in a lot of impulsive behavior and always seemed to be trying to show rather than tell his parents how angry and/or hurt he was. Tony could not at first comprehend that his mother was incapable of understanding him. He also got into wild fights with his then-girlfriend. The two of them would "key" (scratch with a key) one another's cars, throw loud scenes on the street, take one another's most expensive belongings hostage, and so forth. It was the craziest of love affairs, with each partner repeatedly breaking up and then instituting lusty reunions.

Tony would invite his parents to his sessions with me and yell at them full throttle as I desperately tried to restore the scene to a reflective tone. "Talking *only* here!" I would shout. "*Look* at me! You are not allowed to attack anyone but me here in my office." Usually that stopped Tony, because it is not satisfying to attack someone who has not offended you and who doesn't flinch and turn red at every word you say.

I am pleased to report that, after eight years, Tony had become a real patient, by which I mean able to talk about his life with growing awareness and insight. He held a steady job and has seemed to be taking care of himself (aside from one other love affair full of drama). Then suddenly he got into trouble with the law again for the same old reason: his attraction to disturbed, violent women like his mother. One night following a fight (verbal, not physical), his current girlfriend called the police and accused Tony of rape. Again Tony fell into the clutches of the law, and with his prior conviction, this time he faced twenty years in jail if convicted. After several days of calming down, the girlfriend felt remorseful enough to call the police and recant her accusation, but the damage had already been done. The prosecuting attorney refused to drop the charges, having found an old restraining order that the first torrid girlfriend had filed ten years earlier. Apparently, prosecuting a sex offender is too much of a feather in a prosecutor's cap for him to desist.

For several years most of Tony's earnings and a lot of his father's poured into the pockets of his defense lawyer. The courts kept postponing his hearing, probably because they didn't have much of a case, or so my law-enforcement friends told me. Tony lived in terror that his current girlfriend would get into the wrong mood and reinstitute her rape charge. He wooed her and pleaded with her and tried to get her into treatment with me. She accused him of being weak when he flooded her with his tears.

What keeps me going with this roller-coaster soap opera of a family? I think it is that they keep coming and talking to me. Catherine has set my heart racing on a few occasions, screaming wildly at her husband, at Tony, or at me. She knows I will not hesitate to call the police if she goes into action, and so far she has had enough self-control not to blow in my office. I now think of Tony as a thoughtful guy, although I also know he is doomed to keep connecting with women who are beautiful and treacherous the way his mother is. He wants to be therapeutic to them. He wants to work out his early trauma with his mother by having a different outcome with someone like her in the present. Boys want to marry and to cure their mothers, so that is no surprise. I tell him he has emotional intelligence, a talent for my field.

Catherine makes appointments with me, shows up an hour late, and then is furious to be displaced by my next hour's patient and sent home. Yet she says that I am the only one who understands her. My colleagues wonder why I work with such a challenging family—other therapists would have thrown up their hands in despair. But someone has to do it, for all their chaotic behavior. I don't mind being a little bit afraid from time to time. Perhaps I persist in working with them because in doing so I am still working on my *own* trauma. Undoubtedly I am forever curing my own mother.

B. THAT TONE OF VOICE

The emotional communications that most bother me are conveyed by tone of voice:

1. Sneering criticism: "Only a fool would think that!" The tone says, "Your mind is dirt!"

2. A blaming/shaming tone of voice: "Can't you ever think of what others need?" It triggers my guilt regardless of my innocence.

3. A dismissive tone: "Don't bother me now! Can't you see I'm busy doing my nails?" The tone conveys, "You mean nothing to me."

Other than with my patients and students, whom I always encourage to say everything to me (it is what I get paid for), my tolerance for these offensive tones of voice can be limited. If someone says I did a wrong thing, so long as they don't adopt an insidious, accusatory tone, I have no difficulty with it. I do wrong things all the time, and I am always ready to consider mending my ways. Similarly I am okay with being bossed around so long as I am not guilt-tripped or left feeling I cannot say "no." In my experience, relationship issues such as these are self-correcting if we agree to talk (versus accuse or shame one another) about them. (Of course, it is best to cool down first.)

The last trigger—"Go away! Don't bother me now!"—is the most hurtful to me, because it is the quintessential way my mother reacted to me. She is long dead, but someone is always cropping up to remind me of her. Currently it is the woman who mans the desk at my health club. I love to sit in the sauna after my swim, so as I check in I ask, "Is the sauna on?" When she is at the desk, I find it usually is not. She sighs heavily and brushes me off:

"I turned it on this morning. It's on."

"Apparently not," I say. "I just checked."

"Well I don't have time to fix it!" she retorts, her voice awash with annoyance. She sags her shoulders and exhales a burdensome sigh as she swivels her chair so that her back is to me. I dry up into a husk inside. Can the desk clerk tell how easily defeated I am by her antics? Probably not, but she does make me hate her—and myself—at least briefly.

I once had a dramatic exchange with my husband about his tone of voice. I had done something wrong—I can't remember what, something absent-minded, like putting the checkbook in the wrong drawer—and he said to me, "I'm puzzled about why you did that." He didn't *sound* puzzled, he sounded annoyed!

"You sound angry," I said.

"No, I'm just curious. Why would you do that?" But his voice still had that edge!

"You sound quite angry!" I repeated.

Finally he exploded: "Of *course* I'm angry! It was a stupid thing to do!" I felt such relief once his anger came out directly with words instead of with that edgy tone! My husband looked momentarily shame-faced but at the same time satisfied. Acknowledging his anger, he had to give up his fantasy that I had intentionally done the thing that upset him. Underneath, he was expecting me to be perfect, the way a small child magically expects and demands that its mother be perfect. And apparently he had given himself the task of being perfect (never angry), too. For the sake of our relationship, he had to realize that, when I make a mistake, it is not my conscious intent to bother him. (Sigh. I cannot rule out unconscious intent, though in that case my misplacing the item would more likely be intended to hurt myself.)

I notice the way people often think, "Well you made me angry, and therefore you are a bad person, so either get away from me or I have the right to punish you." The problem is, I think that much of the time we aren't even aware of when or how or why we make someone angry. We can get lost in the fog of our own thoughts or griefs, whatever they are, and then do something stupid without the least awareness of how it is going to inflame another person.

I have a psychotherapy student who tends to scare everyone else when he is in a class. "I feel very angry about what you just said," he booms at another student, entirely unaware of the biting tone in his loud, gravelly voice. I feel only a tiny hint of fear, for I know that he is unlikely ever to go into action. Furthermore, for all his size, I know that, inside, he is a hurting three-year-old (his age when he was most traumatized by alcoholic parents), able to make a big roar but still feeling small and vulnerable.

"Mr. P.," I remind him, "there is only one person you are allowed to attack in this room, and that is me."

He nods and says, "Oh, yeah. Okay." But when other students say things that get to him, I watch him inflate like a bellows filling with air, and I give him a look:

"Mr. P.?" I caution.

"Oh, yeah. Okay." But later he confronts me: "How come I don't get to express my feelings like everyone else?"

I educate him once more about my cardinal rule: "Talking is always welcome, but no action. You can talk, but you cannot raise your voice, or use an accusatory tone—which is the same thing— or call anybody a name, or tell him his ideas stink." Three-year-olds cannot always tell the difference, yet Mr. P. is willing—and trying—to catch on.

Mr. Y, another student, is quite brilliant, as paranoid personalities often are. But he cannot understand me when I ask what gets him to drown me (and others) out when he disagrees, which is most of the time. His voice rises in hurt as he overrides my reflective tone. He asserts loudly that I am acting just like all the other females who have a conspiracy against men. I also notice how he can't tolerate my "pointing" anything out. He has complained about how his domineering mother kept him from making his points (symbolic of erections to a little boy), and he has been in protest about this all of his life. Unfortunately his paranoia keeps him from advancing in his training, as he says he wishes to do.

I ask him if he could pretend to listen to others even if he disagrees with them—for the sake of getting what he wants. He turns purple at the idea. His voice rises in distressed amplitude, suffocating mine so that I fall impotent and quiet. I wish I knew how to give him what he needs so that he can get over his early traumatic relationship with his mother.

Then I have the thought: *Perhaps Mr. Y. needs many more repetitions of defeating me and shutting me out.* It makes me recall that this is how someone recovers from a serious trauma. The example of the two-and-a-half-year-old son of a patient of mine once brought this fact home to me. I had read about trauma recovery in books, but seeing it before my very eyes contributed an "aha!" corroboration to that abstract learning process. One day this little boy witnessed his mother being harassed by a psychotic vagrant while they were in a neighborhood playground. His mother bundled him and his toys into his stroller as fast as she could and strode out of the park, but the vagrant followed, shouting abuse and threats in a crazed manner. At some point the vagrant rushed forward and pushed the little boy's mother down before finally running away. End of the incident, except the little boy kept saying, over and over, to anyone and everyone, day and night, "Bad man knocked Mommy down! Bad man knocked Mommy down!" He said it to strangers on the street, to the postman, to the neighbors, to the supermarket checkout clerk, to his grandmother on the phone, over and over and over. The troubled child was too upset to eat, play, relax, or sleep.

"What should I do?" his mother pleaded. Generally, I trust children's minds to take them where they need to go, so I recommended letting him keep doing what he was doing, and wait and see. After another month or two, the child's story began to morph. Ultimately it became a triumphant "I knocked the bad man down!" and with that he recovered his emotional balance. He had conquered his trauma, first through telling his story a zillion times, and then through creating a delusion of magical power for himself. Small children get relief from pretending in order to overcome a trauma they have passively suffered at the hands of another. Think of children who have been frightened when their doctor gave them an inoculation. For days after, they act the role of doctor with everyone in the household, giving them shots in the arm. But don't we all create a delusion for ourselves every day, striding forward into our future as if nothing bad will happen to us, today or ever?

C. LEARNED HELPLESSNESS

I no sooner let myself have an optimistic thought about someone recovering from trauma than I have the opposite thought—that recovery can be all but impossible. The ambivalence of my brain! In research laboratories, many species, even cockroaches, have been shown to fall into total apathy when they are repeatedly traumatized by a painful electrical jolt in a setting from which there is no escape. If this goes on long enough, when the researcher opens an escape route the animals remain inert, ignoring the opportunity to flee. Researchers called this dynamic "learned helplessness," a falling into passivity when they have experienced the odds as insurmountable. It becomes an in-grained expectation for which they develop a passive hopelessness. It helps explain another common manifestation of irrationality.

Like other therapists, I observe how, the earlier in life a child ex-perienced trauma, the more intractable the outcome can be. This is of course what researchers in "learned helplessness" are substantiat-ing—how passive surrender can become an engrained habit. I have seen it in the more severe cases I have worked with over the years. One twenty-two-year-old girl, Heather, demonstrated her failure to thrive by living in a poor and dangerous urban neighborhood. She would often "dumpster dive" for food and clothing, refuse to bathe or launder her clothes, and date only out-of-work, dependent men. Heather is bright and talented, but she throws these gifts aside to maintain an angry dependency on her mother and father, forcing them to bear wit-ness to her depredation of herself, as they had inadvertently forced her to witness their scenes of drunken violence when she was small and helpless. Heather's parents love her as best they can and do not know what to do. What is she saying with her behavior? I believe Heather is retelling the story of how she was tossed aside like a rag doll as they engaged in endless, roaring battles with one another, destroying their home before finally divorcing when she was two and a half years old.

CHAPTER 9

SEXUALITY AND SELF-DISCOVERY

A. A Frightening Pang

WHAT I THINK OF as my first powerful sexual experience occurred when I was ten years old. I was staying for a weekend with my father at his home in Manoa Valley, high on a mountainside above the University of Hawaii. I remember it being a bright, sunny day, and for some reason—perhaps I was resting after lunch—I was alone in a bedroom on the lower floor of the house (something like a basement, as the house was situated on a steeply sloped lot with its main floor on the upper level). I recall suddenly feeling a compelling pang down "there" in the part of my body that my mother called my "places." (The part she was always cautioning me to wash extra clean with plenty of soap.) I had gotten from her tone of voice that it was a dangerous and nasty body part.

Back to what was going on down "there": The insistent, almost achy, feeling seemed to be inside me, but where or what it could be I had no idea. I went into the bathroom and tried to locate it with my fingers, but it was nowhere to be found on the surface areas that I knew from cleaning myself. That was when I discovered that I had an opening that had nothing to do with the one that released my urine. The hole was quite deep, and I could tell that the sensation or pang was coming from inside it. Alarmed but also wildly curious, I got a pencil and poked it in (eraser end first), and sure enough, I touched the right spot. It felt strangely wonderful! But I was at once terrified, embarrassed, and guilt-ridden. I knew I was being a very bad girl, doing something that would cause my mother to scream and scold and hit me. I never told a soul, and thankfully my inaugural hormone spurt quieted down for another several years.

Because I could never talk to my mother about myself as I was growing up, I had to manage such experiences on my own. I didn't know the word for that opening. I had seen a cow and two cats give birth, but I didn't associate those experiences with anything that might go on with my body. I wanted to be a good girl and not talk or even think about forbidden subjects. When my sister, two years older than I, got her first period, I was never told. She and I did not discuss sex comfortably until both of us were well past menopause.

Still, other marvels occurred. At school when I was in fifth grade, relations between the sexes ramped up. We played a thrilling game we called "wild horses" during recess. In this game the stallions chased the mares, trying to herd and catch them as we all made appropriate stamping and whinnying sounds. We fairly flew across the baseball field and up a little embankment into the weeds of a vacant lot. If the boys trapped a girl in their midst, there was would be an attempt by the main stallion to kiss her. I remember one rousing time when it happened to me. The king of the stallions at that time was Reginald, a boy in my class. He was shorter than I, red haired, and covered with freckles, and he was the hands-down champion at "show and tell." His father had been stationed in Alaska for some years, and Reginald mes-merized the rest of us with stories about living in that cold, cold place. I "liked" him, but it was not in the compelling sexual way that I think of as almost like a witch's spell.

Another boy my age, whom I only saw once, kindled that insidious, compelling feeling in me at about that same time period by telling my sister that he "liked" me. Something about the way she reported it made it sound illicit. I had seen the boy, a dark-eyed stranger about my size, hanging out in the playground behind the church up the steep, grassy hill near our house in Annandale, Virginia. I kept finding ex-cuses to return to that playground and couldn't get him out of my mind for months, though I never saw him other than that once.

What I notice about these experiences when I was in fifth grade was that I was already thinking about the differences between the boys in my midst. Bright, verbal Reginald was a boon companion, a civilized kid who got good grades and made our whole class laugh. He was safe and not without appeal in his own way. The other boy, the stranger, excited a wilder side of me, a side that connected sensual stimulation with danger. I sensed that he was the sort of boy I would have to keep a secret from everyone else, someone a "nice" girl would not go near, though I would probably have been willing to, given the opportunity, at least once. Thinking about him triggered a longing of some sort, all because I had heard he "liked" me. It was as if, when it came to this stranger, I was under that witch's spell. But I think, even so, if I had had to make a choice, I would have chosen Reginald and a bright future over the uncertainty of dark and skulking passion.

As a psychotherapist I can see that I was sorting out who I was, what boys were all about, and all the possibilities and choices the world would have to offer. I desperately wanted to be a "nice" girl, which more than anything else meant staying "safe." Yet at eleven I was also on my way to being an adolescent, eager to break free of the strictures of my mother's rules, which may have been what that stranger in the church playground offered. In retrospect I am glad that my mother kept a tight rein on me.

Here is a sampling of my boyfriends: When I was twelve, right about the time I got my first period, we were living on a naval base north of San Francisco, where I attended a local school. Despite my mouthful of braces, I somehow attracted a nice-looking boy in my art class, and he would maneuver to sit next to me in our monthly assembly program. As soon as the lights went out and the credits of yet another ERPI Classroom Film came up, he would surreptitiously take my hand and hold it in his. Nothing else happened, but that handholding was as tender and sensual an experience as any I have ever had.

That fall, when my stepfather got stationed to the Military Mission to the United Nations, we moved to Larchmont, New York. In a few days I began to notice boys my age on bicycles stopping by our new house and asking my sister's and my names, as if word had somehow gotten around town about our arrival. Only one persisted in visiting me, and I didn't like him much, but I did like getting his attention. Another lured me with the promise of an identification bracelet if I would "go steady" with him, but I was incensed that he would think of me as up for barter. The neighborhood boy I did like was a tall, fair-haired comedian named Doug. He would often walk with me the half mile to and from school, and I would be convulsed with laughter the whole way. I was a little afraid of him because of his impulsivity, and I did get into trouble with my English teacher, Miss Van de Water, who told me, "You'd be a better student if you didn't pay so much attention to the boys." Unfortunately, his mother sent him away to a prep school the following year.

A number of other exciting things happened during the two and a half years we lived in Larchmont: I had my first date, which was with a boy whose name I no longer recall, probably because of my anger. He invited me to a dance at the local Methodist church, but when he saw my shoes, he was so offended by their lack of style, he never spoke to me again. I learned from that encounter to beware of boys with snobbish taste. Then I had an exciting series of episodes, along with my older sister, when a pair of boys from the next town over started showing up at our house—one for her, and one for me. She and I were both intrigued, but my mother emphatically disapproved of the way they turned up when we were home alone babysitting for my younger brothers. Apparently our neighbors had snitched on us. Still later, my sister and I took up with two boys whose parents my parents socialized with, so at least they were considered safe. Here is how enterprising they were: They would come to our house, at two in the morning, carrying a ladder, throw a pebble against the window of the bedroom my sister and I shared, and climb up for a clandestine chat and perhaps a bit of snuggling. I felt like Rapunzel letting down her hair, except our boys brought their own access. My father could never figure out what made the strange indentations at the back of his flowerbed.

When I was in tenth grade, we moved to Norfolk, Virginia, where my father attended a war college and then was assigned the captaincy of a missile cruiser docked at Little Creek Naval Station. I attended Princess Anne County High School, located a few miles west of Virginia Beach, a fifteen-mile bus ride from my house. The boyfriends I remember there, especially Body Mumps and Goldbrick, were as wonderful friends as a girl could ever desire. We would talk about everything in our hours-long phone conversations, and I always felt safe and valued in their company. Whatever few beers we drank did not lead to dangerous driving. We had a convention in the South, which both boys and girls followed: It was okay to do everything sexually except have intercourse. We would neck literally for hours on end—our socials and parties were all about "making out." There was the excitement of whether to allow "first base"—touching the breast, "second base"—touching the vagina, and "third base"—intercourse, which I never felt pressured to do, though we did engage in a lot of "humping." Even when I started dating a twenty-year-old from Georgia (and therefore a southern gentleman) who was attending the Naval Academy, I did not feel pressured for intercourse, or not at least until the following year, after he had gone on a training cruise to France and experienced the real thing. After that, he lost his gentlemanly restraint, and I lost my interest in him. My mother offered to get me birth control, but I was not ready to consider doing anything that planned. Somehow I was determined to educate myself in my own cautious, dreamy way. What kind of man did I want? What kind of lifestyle? Living where? Doing what? The one thing I had ruled out was being a stay-at-home mom like my mother.

In short, my adolescent sexual education was consistently sweet. I think our southern custom of refraining from intercourse kept our relationships from becoming obsessive and crazed. Holding back that vital part of ourselves enabled us to experiment with many partners, which was both fun and educational. One or two girls in my high school class got "knocked up" and soon after disappeared, sometimes into early marriage. I literally could not have borne that fate, and might even have been driven mad by it. I was still a half-formed, traumatized girl, not yet fit for independent living, let alone motherhood. Something inside me was missing, a sort of inner gyroscope to keep myself on an even keel. I needed my four years of college, and then some years of independent living, before I would be ready for the choices, demands, and sacrifices of marriage. I didn't capitulate until I was twenty-six, by which time I had figured out a lot about what I wanted: a decent, calm, tolerant, honorable, financially stable man who did not use drugs or alcohol in any serious way and who had an abiding interest in culture and the arts.

I married the chairman of the art department at the high school where I was teaching, a marriage that has lasted to this day. We began our life together as passionate but immature adults who had a lot to learn about intimate communication. With help from the resources of my second education and career in psychotherapy, we have achieved a satisfying life together focused on family and friends, as well as on pursuing our own separate paths of development and creativity.

B. Sexual Education

Sex is still not freely talked about in schools. What is taught in "health class" is mostly the sort of facts that the most conservative parent could tolerate: the basics of menstruation and reproduction, with lots of encouragement to remain celibate until marriage—going so far as getting girls to sign pledges to this effect in some parochial schools. The fear is that, if children are allowed to talk or even think about sex openly, it will lead to rampant promiscuity. I understand parents' fears. Adolescents in their immaturity do not have good judgment, and helping them curb their impulsivity is beneficial. But paradoxically, with their negative suggestibility, the more something is forbidden, the more compulsive it becomes.

I think of the many countries where sex is more accepted and relaxed than here in our own. (Of course, there are also countries where it is far more dangerous and repressed.) I have learned that, in Sweden, for example, an active sex life in adolescence is the norm. Parents accept it, and communities accept it. The thing I wonder about is, why as an adolescent, I associated having intercourse with so much danger. I somehow believed it contaminated a girl, put her at risk for disease, for physical change, for psychological ruin. I thought that she would be darkened emotionally by the experience, that she would lose her ability to fall in love and be devoted to one man. I still have those thoughts about promiscuity. But then the question is, how are we to find out what we like unless we experiment and look around?

Since I could not talk about my adolescent sexual explorations with my mother, I was massively inhibited and distrustful about discussing them with anyone else. To do so publicly in a class at school would have been out of the question. Besides, I was pretty okay with the way things went without adult interference. Yet I think I could have learned a lot that would have helped me survive my fairy tale expectation of living "happily ever after." Having been starved of emotional closeness in my family, I knew little to nothing about how to cope with the conflicts and hidden emotional dilemmas of marriage.

The most important part of a relationship is not sex but communication. Sex gets us together, but then the challenge starts—how to talk when frustrations emerge. If we did not see a good model of intimate communication in our early years, we will be hard-put to achieve it in our own marriage. Further, if we harbor old grievances from our childhood, we will inevitably rediscover them in our current relationships. For example, since my mother never talked to me about feelings and thoughts, silence became my template for intimacy. I expected us each just to *know* what the other needed or felt, and of course I fantasized it would be fine. As I discovered this was not so, I was filled with resentment at my husband and had no way to express it. What was I to do with my frustrated feelings? I spent a lot of time in a sulk, which I think—I hope!—he didn't even notice most of the time.

Then there is the question of how to deal with temptation. What is the value of maintaining faithfulness in marriage? Why not have an "open marriage," or live a life of serial divorces, or dispense with monogamy altogether? As a grandparent I have one tremendously important answer to these questions: Besides my husband, who else on this planet could ever adore my children and grandchildren as much as I do? This means everything to me. And I have seen at first hand what the statistics show: Divorce devastates children, damaging their belief in true love and their optimism about the future. It also typically impoverishes the mother. Nonetheless, I acknowledge that it is preferable to murder.

The one thing that I know for sure is that talking is beneficial in every relationship and at every stage of life. Certainly every teen should learn and discuss the dangers of sexually transmitted diseases. Avoiding such talk does not stop young people from doing what their biology impels them to do. Rather, it forces them into a mind frame in which they delude themselves by thinking, "Those things won't happen to me." Our Puritan ancestors understood the dilemma of premarital sexuality, permitting young people of courtship age to spend the night together with a "bundling board" between them. I imagine the young people had a wonderful time, and probably quite a few hastened their union by jumping the barrier. But those were times when most people anticipated having relatively short, predictable lives consisting of drudgery and hardship. They did not have the expectation of today's youth that their years of carefree dependency could extend indefinitely into the future, until the crashing moment when they realize it will not. Postponing facing up to adulthood may have some benefits, but our biology intends for us to have our children while we are still young. Some birth defects are now found to be associated with the aging germ cells of ova and sperm. This is a dilemma.

c. The Imperative to Break Free

Working as a therapist with young adolescents, I find they urgently need to talk about their relationships with their parents. Compared to that, peer relationships and sex are minor. Since the emotional task of adolescence is to separate and individuate in preparation for adulthood, teens engage in a powerful love/hate interaction with their parents. Simultaneously, teens go into a regression, a funk, which seems to accompany any maturational spurt. They often act in many ways like two-year-olds—messy, stubborn, selfish, and defiant—instead of like near-adults. Since this is biological, we have to accept and manage it with good grace. These powerful dynamics fuel the surreptitious "Go ahead and try to make me do what you want—it isn't going to work" games of doing the things their parents forbid them to do. Yet notice that the games are meaningless without their parents feeling impotent and enraged in the background.

Here I want to plug the benefit of having an emotionally educated person available to help teens talk about their many conflicts. Annie, for example, began working with me in her second semester of college, referred by her mother because she had begun "delicately cutting" herself with a razor on the underside of her upper arms. Annie had fallen into a pall of hopelessness, rage, and despair. Her relationship with her father had been clouded ever since her parents' divorce when she was five. She was heartbroken and enraged at him for disappearing from her life, for his remarrying and having four more children, and above all for his general inability to relate to her, albeit he remained a devoted provider. Annie was also furious at her mother, who was showing signs of incipient alcoholism. Her father is not a good communicator, which has affected Annie's choice of boyfriends. Forget Annie's enjoying her sexual rebellion. Since neither parent was emotionally able to take notice, it didn't count.

Annie and her boyfriend enrolled in the same college, but what had been a mutually supportive relationship in high school went sour as her boyfriend became possessive and demanding. She broke off with him, but he pursued her to the point of stalking her. She felt guilty and frightened and lost. After talking about these concerns for a few months and getting my consistent emotional support, Annie stopped the cutting. Talking became the substitute outlet for her unbearable inner tension. Essentially, I educated her that all her feelings made perfect sense.

Nonetheless, her worries, particularly about her parents, did not lessen, primarily because, like oldest siblings, Annie was the responsible one in the family. She had taken on the role of mother's helper when she was quite small. One of her brothers, and a sister, even enrolled in her college so as to continue to depend on her for emotional and financial sustenance. (She held a job, and they didn't!) Annie's greatest conflict was between being responsible for them and wishing to devote herself to her own needs. Even her grandparents leaned on her emotionally. I saw a major part of my task as freeing her from this hyper-responsible role, to whatever extent possible (no one gives up such lifelong habits readily). She also needed to muster the optimism necessary to succeed in her chosen field (a highly competitive one) despite the chaos back at home.

Talking to me, Annie sounded whiny and hopeless. Anything I said, she rejected as useless. She considered my questions annoying. I had the thought that she needed to defeat me in order to feel victorious, as a girl needs to defeat her mother. Nonetheless she attended her sessions with me regularly. As I listened, I wondered if she needed to infuse me with the suffering she wanted her mother to feel as a mirror to her own. Acting like her narcissistic twin, I modeled how to suffer and soldier on.

True to form, Annie's current boyfriend leans on her heavily. He gets enraged when he sees her writing a text message on her cell phone, jumping to the conclusion that she is preparing to cheat on him. He wants her to spend every spare moment with him. When she engages in interests and activities of her own, he sulks and binges on alcohol. She has found someone who resembles both her mother (the alcohol use) and her father (the moodiness and withdrawal when he feels she is failing to understand his needs). She acknowledges that her boyfriend is paranoid and narcissistic. He wants her to read his mind and abandon herself to him. He jealously suspects that another, younger boy is interested in her, which happens to be true. She, on the contrary, believes he should be pleased that she has stuck by him. Like all of us, she has to figure out what to do about her propensity to choose someone needy like her parents. It is the natural outcome of her emotional underpinnings. She was not faintly aware of having this dynamic until I recently questioned her about it. She hopes against hope that her boyfriend will just wake up one day and see her for who she is. She has to learn by experience that this is not going to happen. I ask whether he should be in therapy, but she says it is not her place to make such a suggestion.

D. EMIL: A HOPELESS CASE

Boys usually end up in therapy when their parents panic about their school performance. This was true of Emil, who was fourteen when he was referred to me. Both his parents, and Emil himself, believed his life would not be worth a crumb if he did not get into a good college. However, he had been a miserable failure since kindergarten. His parents wondered if he had Asperger's autism or some other neurological malady. In middle school he had been in a special education program for students with emotional problems. His psychiatrist had diagnosed him as suffering from Attention Deficit Disorder (ADD) and Attention Deficit Hyperactive Disorder (ADHD), and prescribed Ritalin. But when Emil graduated from the special education middle school, his parents could not find another suitable placement for him, so they enrolled him in a nearby large neighborhood high school, hoping for the best. Instead, as usual, Emil failed completely, and his parents received many phone calls from upset teachers. Thinking about Emil's parents' goal for him, I felt skeptical. The objective of his getting into a "good" college struck me as a stretch. As it turned out, my three years of working with him stretched me.

Emil had no friends. He was not malicious, at least not on the surface, but goofy and very impulsive. At school he once jumped out of his seat and rushed toward his teacher, badly frightening her. It turned out his intent had been to drop to his knee and plead his case to her—something about handing in homework late—in a highly dramatic way.

In sessions with me he was passive-aggressive. He said he had nothing to say. He said he could never talk to me because I was a total stranger. He said he could never trust me. He complained of boredom. He told me to ask him questions and then gave one-word answers. His actions, however, spoke volumes. He would play with his cell phone. He would play with his game boy and his Ipod. He would play with objects in my office, tossing them in the air. He tossed up a red silk pillow, narrowly missing the whirling ceiling fan. I could only think about what would happen if the pillow connected with its blades. He tossed my desk clock from hand-to-hand and then up in the air, over and over, as I would repeat, "Hey, could you put that in words? We're only supposed to talk here." It was clear Emil didn't want to be with me, and he let me know it each time we met. Although I never scold or try to pressure my patients, I found myself dreading his sessions and wondering whether I could stick it out with this boy.

Then one day he announced upon entering my office, "You know, I've been acting like an asshole because I hoped that would get you to throw me out."

"Look," I replied, "I don't mind your acting like an asshole, but could you do it in *words?* Here we are only supposed to talk." But already I felt relieved. Once a patient starts talking, they stop having to dramatize what is going on in their mind.

Emil began telling me about his summer camp, which specialized in music. Sounding forlorn, he spoke about how girls would come to his cabin, where he sat on the porch in the evening, and ask him the whereabouts of other boys.

He spoke about how his father had bought him a new computer but then used it himself, filling its memory with music that he downloaded from the Internet. He told me his computer was kept in his sister's room because there was not enough room in his own. (She was away at college.) When I expressed shock at this arrangement, he looked surprised. He revealed that he is treated like someone far younger than his age. He is not allowed to make his own decisions, such as choosing what clothing he would like to buy and wear. I learned that his older sister was an academic superstar, seemingly perfect in every way, whereas he, Emil, was "a good for nothing."

In addition to meeting with Emil, I met regularly with his parents, mainly his mother. Her speech was pressured and mostly about herself. I was unable to engage in a discussion with her about Emil, because she was too consumed with the need to discuss her own career. I realized that, to help her pay more attention to him, I needed to pay more attention to her. She spoke about putting together a portfolio and hiring a professional to help her. Later she got angry at the professional and refused to pay him what she had promised. It did not surprise me that, not long thereafter, I found myself having to wait for months and months to get paid by her.

The second year, Emil continued to complain about having to come. I asked him, "What should I do?"

"Tell her I don't have to come."

"What will convince her?"

"Well, I have to get good grades. And I have to make sure teachers don't call home complaining about me." Then he fell silent. We both realized we were stuck with each other for a while.

One day after an exchange with me, Emil gave me "the finger," and I told him, "Put it in words."

"Okay, fuck you," he said, looking up to see how I would react.

"That's better," I said.

Unexpectedly, Emil strode into my office one day and announced that he had gotten a role in the school play. I soon began to notice a sea change in his talk—he was sounding enthusiastic about school! Subsequently he got a role in another play and also began learning to do backstage work such as lighting and set design. He would perform for me, either singing a song in his promising tenor voice, or acting out some lines or a comedic bit. I began to find myself laughing at frequent intervals. The torture began to drain out of our relationship. We were both enjoying ourselves.

Emil often arrived at his session without any money to pay for his subway fare home, and I would have to lend him some. I still thought of him as more like a ten-year-old than a fifteen- year-old. At the end of the second year, he got one or two good grades but still he complained about academics. Disciplined study was not his thing. He did not like to learn, and that was that. But what astonished both his parents and me was that he got high marks on his regents' exams, including one for a class that he had failed. Emil was exposing his considerable intelligence!

The third year, Emil continued to grumble about having to come to see me but still arrived on time for his sessions. He spoke about his parents' opposition to his interest in science fiction. They didn't like him to play his magic game at the card store, either. If he didn't hide his Pokemon cards, his mother would confiscate them and throw them away. His father would walk into his room without knocking to check on him. He assumed I would support these behaviors by his parents and was surprised—and intrigued—when, instead, I was aghast! I gave Emil a tirade about the sacredness of privacy and private property.

He began to be a bit more interested in me. "Are you married?" he asked. I was glad to hear him beginning to sound more interested in sex, more like someone his own age. By the third year he had grown six inches and filled out around his shoulders and chest. Honing his acting skills, he began demonstrating them for me. For example, when I opened my office door for him to enter, he might step forward and then dramatically pause to recite the lines from a scene in his latest play. I'd applaud, and we'd both laugh.

He also began to share his secrets. He was very interested in playing a science fiction game that year, and he would stop at a bookstore that sold game supplies on his way home. His mother did not want him to do those things, so he was becoming rebellious—a real teenager—at last. I welcomed his telling me this, for it showed his mounting trust in me.

Emil's father came in with him, complaining that Emil had been disrespectful, and that he would have to punish him. We had a discussion about Emil's impudence, and when I told his father this was normal behavior for an adolescent, the man seemed relieved. I could see that Emil appreciated hearing that he was a normal kid.

Emil's report cards showed him passing every subject except French. His father was most impressed with his getting an "A" in chemistry. None of his teachers had called home about him for ages. Emil suffered a disappointment when he didn't get the lead in the next school play, but he did get a very good supporting role. His friends had been sure he would get the lead, but he was just not quite the straight-laced type the role called for. (Now he *had* friends!) He was planning to take his SATs soon. He began talking about what college he might like to go to, mentioning several good, small colleges. His mother's new worry was why he didn't have a date for the senior prom. And, yes, he finished his senior year having been accepted at several good colleges.

What worked in Emil's treatment? Like so many of the children who wind up in my office, Emil had not gotten adequate narcissistic mirroring. Though both of his parents have very attractive qualities and are devoted to their children, on closer look they are both very needy themselves. Dad buys him a computer and then hogs it for his own use. Emil was too compliant to protest. Was it "learned helplessness?" Mom had been so wound up in her ideas of what is needed to succeed in this world that she hadn't been able to notice Emil's talents. Instead she gave herself the task of forcing him to fit her own mold.

She had based her life on a scholastic record that enabled her to get an excellent higher education. Emil cannot be his mom, but he sure can be himself: an actor, a rebel, a charmer, and when he is not forced, a good learner.

What had Emil's "pall" been about? Why had his mother concluded that his was a hopeless case of learning disability? I know what made him better (the relationship with me), but I can only hypothesize about what in his history led to his stubborn refusal to succeed in school. An anxious, dominating mother, a disappointing father who kowtowed to her, an older sibling who was an academic superstar—I speculate that these were among the influences that led to Emil's adopting a "loser" role for himself. His defense was passive-aggressive. Outwardly compliant, he got his revenge through being a lifelong failure. Beneath the surface, he had been doing what many children do—shooting himself in the foot instead of unloading his misery on his parents. He knew they were too tense and volatile to tolerate hearing what he needed to say. Instead I helped him tell it to me, even if he did it at first through his actions. Though he put me to the test, he did it within a limit I could endure. Aside from testing me as by trying to get me to throw him out, he was basically courteous to me. Teens have a desperate need to feel liked, even when they feel unlikable, so that was expectable. His need to see himself in a better light filtered through me.

Children succeed to please their mothers, but his mother was unreachable because of her anxiety and the life-long rut they had gotten into together. But he sure could please me—just by not breaking my clock, by not actually hitting the fan with my pillow, by coming regularly, by testing me in nonverbal ways rather than ignoring me, increasingly by entertaining me, and then passing those Regents exams! How hard did I laugh hearing that!

As a psychotherapist I see evidence of success in the results I get. But I cannot pinpoint all of the complex events that occur in a child's mind to comb out his tangled web of conflict. One way I think of it is that, in a close relationship, we become one another, so by becoming me he got some of my strength, optimism, and flexibility. I got the joy of seeing him grow into a talented performer, a backstage technician, and a capable student. As he developed, his parents began to recognize his potential, which augmented his upward spiral.

Psychotherapy has been called "the talking cure." Actually it should be called the *listening* cure, if we are talking about the therapist's role. We help people talk by listening carefully and asking the right questions, so that there is more talk. When children experience the important adults in their lives as considerate, respectful, and empathetic, they want to be considerate, respectful, and empathetic in return. Children feel important when they are heard. This helps them dare to become themselves. We help them talk when we consistently affirm their feelings. When we help children keep an eye on their own goals and help them weigh all the ramifications of their decisions in terms of their goals, we help them develop their ability to deal with reality.

CHAPTER 10

UNIVERSAL EMOTIONAL TRUTHS

A. "AND NOW A WORD FROM OUR SPONSOR"

I AM AN ADVOCATE of continuous, lifelong, emotional education. This means exercising our minds through ongoing, reflective discussion with others and with ourselves about our feelings. Reading thoughtful writing on the subject of passions, moods, and terrors supplements such talk. Without this expansion of ourselves through speaking and thinking together, we become prone to states of inner tension that sap our energy and menace our health. Every day I listen to people, not just my students and patients, but my family members, my buddies at my health club, my colleagues at my training institute, and my neighbors and acquaintances, both young and old. All need to talk—about their anxieties, their annoyances, their self-doubts, their relationships and passions, and their sufferings.

Emotionally, we are all prone to getting tied in knots. As children we had no perspective on the emotional conflicts we suffered. Without the emotional education of psychotherapy, most adults do not either. Instead they feel insulted or betrayed or just exhausted by how difficult other people in their lives can be. They also often assume there is something uniquely wrong with them, or else wrong with their spouse, their mother, their boss, their. . .someone. They have no inkling that other people endure the same tormented dramas as they do at home or school or work. Most do not even have the language to describe their inner life. They do not know that a tormented mind is part of being human. They do not know that talking is the best way to diminish and relieve feelings of misery. This is tragic.

How can free and open awareness and discussion of feelings be made more of a daily event? In this chapter I will explore classical literature for the remarkable emotional awareness that our long ago forbearers developed. Stories become classics when they portray the universal truths that speak to the dilemmas of being human. It seems the ancients wanted to understand and teach, too.

B. TRIUMPH AND TRAGEDY: CUPID AND PSYCHE, OEDIPUS, MEDEA, AND NARCISSUS

Cupid and Psyche

I begin with a story of successful love: Cupid and Psyche. Though it by no means portrays unalloyed, pure, or uncomplicated love, theirs is the archetypal Greek myth of marriage. Psyche means "soul," and in her story the ancient writers exemplified their observation that being a human soul is very challenging. It seems we cannot live or love without hate shadowing us along the way.

Their story begins as Psyche is honored as Maiden of the Year by her village. Her reward is to be taken to a mountaintop and thrown off—sacrificed—to ensure that the crops will grow. Hate from parental symbols, albeit cleverly disguised, even from themselves, is present from the start. Envy of the beautiful maiden aroused their homicidal impulses. Free falling to her death, she is rescued by Cupid, god of love. Her ability to attract a stranger enables her to survive the ill will of the older generation.

Cupid carries her to his dark cave, where they become lovers. However, he warns Psyche that she cannot look at him, a rule instituted by his all-powerful mother, Aphrodite, goddess of love, famous for her envy of other women's beauty. (The potential destructiveness of the older generation, as represented by a jealous and interfering mother-in-law, appears again.) Soon Psyche visits her sisters to tell them of her happiness, but teasing her about not knowing what her lover looks like, her sisters tempt her to break the rule. (Envying Psyche's happiness they instigate her to self-destruct.) Psyche lights a candle one night to behold her sleeping husband's handsome face, and a drop of hot wax falls on his wing, wakening him. Instantly they must part. (The honeymoon crashes as the young couple takes a closer look at each other, and he opts for his mother over her.) But then Cupid implores his mother to relent. She finally agrees, provided that Psyche completes some impossible tasks.

Given the impossibility of what she assigns, Aphrodite humors her son while protecting herself from losing him to the mortal stranger. However, she fails to anticipate Psyche's ability to persevere. After years of sacrifice and toil, Psyche manages to complete the tasks and succeeds in winning back her man. Together at last, they have a child named "Pleasure."

Condensed in Psyche's story are the many hazards of reaching adulthood. Repeatedly she is faced by the treachery of the older generation. Further, getting married is like a death, spelling the end of carefree childhood. (Some marital partners never forgive their spouses for separating them from their mothers and burdening them with the drudgery of adulthood and parenthood.) Psyche's story shows above all that enduring love requires a lot of hard work.

The injunction against Psyche's looking at her lover echoes the Biblical story of the Garden of Eden, when Eve was forbidden to eat the fruit from the tree of knowledge. What is so dangerous about knowing the truth? Both stories emphasize the danger of doing so, but then, many partners feel betrayed when they emerge from the intoxication of new love. Like Eve, Psyche breaks a commandment. All children feel they are in some way betraying their parents as they go off into their own lives. Both Psyche and Eve are banished for daring to develop their own identities through gaining knowledge. This is the terrible price they must pay for breaking free of childhood. Yet there is the promise of a reward once the difficult work is done. We achieve pleasure and a sort of immortality through having a child. It is not a purely happily-ever-after scenario, but neither is reality.

Our psyche is our soul. Psyche's story shows that the worst dangers arise in the very relationships that are meant to nurture us. A stranger rescued her at the moment when the village elders, her symbolic parents, were attempting to kill her. Her only crime was being young and beautiful. As children we all experienced murderous responses in our home environment, often done in the guise of it being "for our own good," or because God commanded it, as in the Genesis story of Abraham and Isaac. Beauty, charm, and innocence are our childhood riches, our payment in kind for obtaining the attention and care we need, but they are not an impenetrable armor. Inevitably we face hatred and betrayal.

Psyche aroused the homicidal impulses of her community and later of her mother-in-law. Teens typically arouse a lot of anger with their steamy sexuality, defiance, and posturing. Taking a better look at her beloved in the candlelight menaces Psyche's marriage. But why did Cupid uphold his mother's arrogant decree instead of allowing his wife to look at him? The dependency tie to the parent is too powerful, too opposed to maturing into independence and adulthood. These are the conflicts that threaten intimacy. The marital bedroom is crowded with the residue of family loyalty, dependency, idealism, and betrayal.

Psyche was a mortal dealing with immortals, hinting at the anxiety we feel around new in-laws. When we awaken from early infatuation, we face the hard task of getting along with powerful, dangerous strangers. We discover that marriage is based on endless labor. Through perseverance we may attain adulthood and pleasure, if we survive. But the hazards are many, and it takes forever. Ultimately Psyche's success derives from pure grit and determination.

Oedipus' Swollen Foot

Oedipus unwittingly ends up killing his father and marrying his mother. Here Freud found corroboration for his observation that every child's first and truest love is his mother. (For the girl child, this love in time may shift to the father, at least in part.) Throughout our lives we unwittingly try to recapture what we felt as infants. Mother/father, or rather unconscious, dream-like traces of them, is whose love and devotion we really crave. In infancy we experienced mother/father as god-like, magical, and perfect. Any mere mortal could never live up to their standard in our inmost fantasy. When we are young we have enough passion to fly over the barriers of doubt into marriage, but the ancient Greeks wanted to alert us to love's inevitable disappointments and threats.

Yet, wait. Freud left out an important detail in his study of Oedipus' problems. It was that Oedipus' parents, in response to the prophesy of a roadside beggar, tied his heels together and exposed him to die on a mountaintop to die. (The name "Oedipus" translates as "swollen foot.") Adoptive parents, not his biological ones, raised him. Clearly, the ancient Greeks had noticed the murderous feelings parents can have toward their offspring. Further, they connected abandonment in infancy with the madness of homicidal and incestuous behavior in adulthood. There was more to Oedipus's tragedy than just undying love for his mother. His patricide resulted from his infantile trauma. This is something we must think about if we are to understand the complications of intimacy. All of us to some extent or other were traumatized.

Medea: Marital Break Up, Murder, and Infanticide

Medea portrays the homicidal rage of a scorned wife. When her husband, Jason, leaves her to marry the king's daughter, Medea goes on a rampage, first murdering their two children, then his new bride, and finally Jason himself. Divorce can create a powerfully negative form of intimacy, one even more compelling than the love that brought about the original union. Like it or not, a couple are joined for a lifetime in nurturing, or avoiding nurturing, or preventing one another from nurturing, or colluding in the destruction of their offspring. The connection and the tension it arouses will always be there. And the children will always be sacrificial lambs for their parents' unresolved wrath. Divorce typically sets off a vendetta, with the partners fighting over finances, possessions, and the loyalty of the kids. It might be best for couples to work out their differences and stay together for the sake of the children. At the very least, they have to continue rearing them cooperatively in order for the children to thrive. Anything else damages them grievously, yet how impossible this proves to be.

Both my own personal history and my profession make the subject of divorce of intense interest to me. Since my parents parted ways when I was four, I have first-hand knowledge of its devastating effects on a child. My mother told me that conceiving me had been a last-ditch attempt to save their marriage, and it had failed. I felt I myself got divorced—from everybody. I was embarrassed to face my father's side of the family, assuming they couldn't help but hate me after my mother had treated him so shabbily. Besides, I saw them so seldom I always felt like an alien intruder. On my rare visits I had to be reintroduced to my own aunts, uncles, and cousins. With my mother's relatives I felt that I couldn't mention my father's name. I felt I shared his status of *persona non grata*, and of course he was no longer around for me to lean against his solid, hearty presence. I felt I had become an embarrassment wherever I went, a footnote to a mistake.

"Love is grand, and divorce is a hundred grand," goes one quip. But the cost extends beyond money to the price of shattering children's lives and the creation of a new class of poverty in single mothers. It is a source of major stress for the principal players, their extended families, and their friends as well. How is it that a relationship that seems to begin in such hope and joy can go so wrong? Of course, the operative word in this last sentence is "seems."

Though I am a survivor of over forty years of marriage, I still sometimes wonder if permanent commitment makes sense. My parents' divorce modeled that love does not last. Biologists have confirmed that the hormone of attachment, oxytocin, only persists for about four years. What could possibly hold two people together for a lifetime? One important answer, in my experience, is that my husband is my devoted friend, as I am his. There is such comfort in coming home to someone who will listen to me and help me in my pursuits, as I listen to and help him with his. I am also grateful that I have stayed the course, because breaking up my marriage and home would have absorbed endless amounts of time and energy that I have preferred using for other pursuits.

Our current culture models easy couplings and partings. It no longer provides much by way of religious or societal censure to oblige us to stay the course. In the mania of punishing one another via divorce, it is easy to avoid taking a good look at all the possible consequences. Do we need some replacement for societal pressure to protect our young and our social stability? How else is the sacred bond of parenthood, so necessary to a child, to be maintained? The approach espoused in a democracy is education. Would it help if we were taught in school about the way things really are in intimacy, the only way we can expect them to be: flawed, bewildering, disappointing, intolerable, enraging, as well as the opposite—comforting, fruitful, and supportive? The Greek heroine Cassandra had the gift of predicting the future, yet she also had the curse of knowing that nobody would listen to her. Is it Cassandra-like to wonder whether, if these emotional realities were taught and freely discussed in school, they would be handled more thoughtfully in adult life? Could we become less impetuous and vicious when frustrations arise?

It is clear to me that most of the destructive ways people deal with one another result from emotional ignorance and unresolved past traumas from their early lives. Although no one has ever met anyone approaching his ideal of an all-loving, all-forgiving, totally trustworthy, considerate, romantic, sexually exciting, industrious, entertaining, nurturing, and cooperative partner, somehow we all harbor the notion that, somewhere out there, one does exist. What a burden the expectation of true love places on relationships.

Personally, having been in therapy groups, and having run therapy groups for many years, including those with my inner-city students, I found I could fall in love with almost anyone once I got to know his or her story well. I could not help but admire and empathize with the heroism exerted by each individual in creatively surviving the destructive forces in his or her life. Understanding and accepting one another constitutes intimacy, a bond that grows with the years. Intimacy stimulates feel-good hormones in our brains and inspires us to thrive and want to create and give something to others and to the civilization that surrounds us.

Narcissus: Unable to Love and Unable to Live

The psychology of someone who is unable to love is portrayed in the Greek myth of Narcissus. From the fact that Narcissus was born of a rape, we can infer that his mother had a feeling of hatred toward her impregnator. In turn this must have made her feel ambivalent and hateful toward the fetus in her womb. Under these circumstances, might the mother's feelings somehow eat at the fetus? Might they create a toxic undercurrent to his sense of self? The molecules of emotions do cross the placental barrier, infiltrating the fetus with what his mother feels. Might this create traces of bitterness somewhere in his brain? And as usual, weren't the ancient writers talking about an aspect of all of us? Haven't we all suffered from our mothers' ambivalence to some degree? Aren't we all retarded in our ability to love ourselves (or others) as a result?

Narcissus' story portrays him as wandering around aimlessly until, kneeling by a pool, he sees his face reflected on its surface. He at once becomes totally absorbed in studying this image, as if that had been what he had been searching for all his life. What did he see? What could he see but himself looking back with equal intensity? Lacking an external nurturer, Narcissus had to find it in himself. But since, emotionally, he was an infant, he was not up to the task. The only human being Narcissus could tolerate was the nymph Echo, another mirror. Like an abandoned newborn, Narcissus died of exposure to the elements. But the myth does not end there—a final detail has him turned into the narcissus plant, a poisonous bulb with a beautiful, trumpet-shaped flower. This is the model of unhealthy narcissism, a condition in which one is poisonous to oneself and to others, however exquisite on the surface.

A conventional reading of this myth has been that Narcissus' was a case of self-love and vanity. But this interpretation, perhaps because it is meant to scold adolescents for being preoccupied with their looks, fails to acknowledge the danger in his obsession. Narcissus' self-neglect led to his death! His final transformation into a poisonous bulb stresses that he was toxic, not only to himself, but to others as well. The inability to make or sustain an intimate connection is a sign of a poisonous process that can damage others as well as the self. Narcissus' fatal behavior was about self-hatred, not self-love.

C. Scenes from Narcissistic Marriages

A patient, Ruth, comes to mind here, for hers is a story of a narcissistic marriage. She had come into psychotherapy because of her fear of her dangerously disturbed boyfriend. Fortunately, at the ninth hour she rejected him. She had a job that enabled her to stay isolated from contact with other people, but the ticking of her biological clock impelled her to connect with another man she barely knew. However, it is likely she intuited that he was as narcissistic, as both her parents had been, and as she herself was. Together these two difficult, narcissistic people had a beautiful baby. Ruth suffered through the years of her marriage more often than not in cold, silent fury. Sexual intimacy mostly consisted of his masturbating until she guiltily took over for him. Astonishingly, this seemed to be the right lifestyle for Ruth, allowing her to maintain her mistrustful isolation.

As time went by, she reported starting to like her husband a little. She accounted for this by the fact that, when she joined a therapy group, she met some men whom she found even more detestable than her husband. It may be that, by the group giving her other men to loathe, her need to focus all of her frustration on her husband lessened. She reported one day that her husband got on top of her during sex, and she had been thrilled for days.

The origin of Ruth's narcissism was illuminated when she took her baby to visit her mother. The baby sat in its infant seat on the kitchen counter while Ruth and her mother prepared dinner. When the baby began to coo sweetly, grandmother strode over and cooed back. But grandmother's loud and callous coo overrode the baby's tender voice, and the infant stopped vocalizing. In this way Ruth was able to observe how her mother's narcissism led to her subtly obliterating others. It is likely that her mother had similarly drowned out Ruth when she was an infant. A memory from when Ruth was a little girl of six indicates that this was so: Ruth's mother would habitually answer questions that were addressed to Ruth as if Ruth herself were not there. And now, decades later, Ruth's mother could not tolerate letting her grandchild have a voice. Like Narcissus, those who have not achieved positive self-intimacy are unable to respect the needs of others. Forever restless, their hunger and anxiety prevent them from recognizing that others are important to them.

The rub is, along a continuum all of us are narcissistic. It creates an unending force for divisiveness in intimacy. At the mild end of the continuum, we all withdraw at times like Narcissus, avoiding others, giving us a needed break. But at the far end of the continuum, our intolerance for a nonmirroring partner is a major contributor to marital breakup. Harmony can only prevail if couples work through their differences, to the point where they can agree not to agree. This is mature functioning.

The classics of world literature describe variations on narcissistic dynamics. Don Quixote, protagonist of the first novel in western literature, is a patrician knight who, among many adventures, falls in love with Dulcinea, a common prostitute. With his poor vision he projects onto her his fantasy of an ideal lady, recreating her in his own likeness, despite her incredulous protestations. It is his narcissistic projection that is his beloved, not the pathetic slattern of reality, but he is too blind and deluded to tell the difference. It makes for many comic moments. Don Quijote represents love as the narcissistic illusion of a needy old man with failing eyes and ears.

D. DEPRESSION AND MARRIAGE

Because the depressive's brain predicts rejection, abandonment, and misery, a self-fulfilling prophecy that hijacks intimacy is created. To a depressive, it feels more natural to suffer defeat than to triumph. Therapists have all worked with depressed patients who repeatedly fall in love, treat their love partner with great sweetness, and then feel betrayed when the loved one does not reciprocate in kind. One woman noticed this in herself: "I keep falling in love with a picture in my head, not the guy himself. Why am I so stupid?" What keeps people in such a painful pattern is their hope that someday they will meet someone who will give them the special love and devotion they never got their fill of in infancy. Depressives tend to have an inability even to ask for what they want. Further, they believe that asking would ruin the feeling they seek; after all, a true love would know what is wanted without being asked. But in reality only the mother of an infant is able to intuit what her child needs, and even then not always. One depressed young man reported that he would not burden his wife by asking her to buy the kind of food he enjoys. Meanwhile he lost weight, embodying Narcissus's self-neglect.

E. COMPLAINING AND MAINTAINING THE STATUS QUO

The grievances we therapists hear daily reflect ignorance of what can be realistically expected of a partner. Complaining is a way of preserving a melancholy feeling of neglect and abandonment first experienced long ago. Sometimes we need to spend time ruminating about how unkind life has been to us. This can feel comforting, but there is really only one way to get what we want from a spouse, which is to find friendly ways to ask, and to keep on asking, until the right way is found to meet our needs. It requires negotiating around the reality of our own resentments (which we rather enjoy), as well as the reality of our partner's. Any other approach keeps us in a bubble of delusion, vainly expecting a miracle as we whine about it not coming. One tried-and-true method of sustaining intimacy is to give a compliment at the very moment when we want to give a criticism. This always gets a positive result, if only we are willing, which in my experience we generally are not, especially if our emotions are aflame.

Annette and Gerry are far enough along in self-awareness to realize that each is the cause of his/her own misery. They try not to inflict their irritations and moods on one another. Neither has the expectation that he or she is responsible for the other's happiness. Their interests are totally separate. Their demands on one another have dwindled as their children have grown and left home. So what is left? Were they not so comfortable in their domestic arrangements and so devoted to their grandchildren, would they drift apart? Though the intense spark of their younger years is gone, sex is still good on occasion. They still find one another smart and interesting. Each feels the quest for a new, more exciting partner is delusional. They both know that to sever their connection to one another would be an exercise in emotional and financial devastation. Force of habit and a mature grasp of reality prevail.

F. TRUE LOVE? HAH!

Samuel Pepys, the noted seventeenth-century English diarist, described his wife's efforts to keep him faithful as becoming increasingly erratic as the years went by. Where at first she and he talked about his peccadilloes with the result that he kept resolving to control himself, she later became obsessed, checking him in the middle of the night to see if he had an erection. If he did, she hysterically demanded to know whom he was dreaming about. Alas, Mrs. Pepys was struggling to protect the notion she had of true love, but since everyone has sexual fantasies about others, the point of faithful intimacy is to restrict actions, not fantasies. Dreams, fantasies, and wishes cannot be contained.

There is no unconditional love. It is the nature of loving feelings to be entwined with hateful ones. The opposite of love is indifference, not hate. Feelings are not a problem if we know we do not have to act on them. Only actions can be restricted, if we are willing to invest

some self-awareness, willingness, and hard work. Our unconscious infantile self wants it all, and without effort, cost, or accountability. We
have to manage our narcissism and we have to cope with our partner's.
These are the dilemmas of intimacy.

G. THE LOVE LIFE OF PORCUPINES

Esther, a young therapist, is learning that, in order to build her
marriage, she needs to understand and talk to her husband in a similar
way to the approach she uses with a patient. An early issue was that
her husband wanted to spend all of his free time with his parents, who
lived several hours away by car. As she told me about his father's tyrannical ways, her husband's guilt-ridden ties to his parents became understandable. Her father-in-law's pathological narcissism emerged in
repeated anecdotes about how he couldn't tolerate her or her husband
having a different opinion from his. One morning when she visited
him at their home in the suburbs, her father-in-law saw her outside
wearing a jacket zipped up to her chin. "Are you cold?" he asked.

"Brrr, yes!"

"Come on, it's not cold! Why don't you unzip your jacket?" If he
wasn't cold, she couldn't possibly be.

In a similar vein he wanted her husband to buy a leather jacket.
"I don't want one," her husband insisted.

"What are you talking about? Everyone in the family is getting
one." His father would not take "no" for an answer.

This time her husband held the line: "No, no, no!"

The next thing they knew, his father bought him one. "It looks
terrific on you," he said. The pattern of a father who cannot tolerate
having his son individuate is clear.

There was considerable anxiety behind his father's narcissistic intolerance, which Esther's husband sensed. He said that he wanted to see his parents as much as possible, because he wouldn't always have them around. Since, at that time, his parents were both under sixty and in good health, his apprehension could only be explained by some uncomfortable feelings fueling his fantasies of their imminent death. Since people are consistent over the years, it is likely that his father had trained him to be wary of disagreeing all his life. Children are attentive to their parents' hidden needs, and seek to protect them. This might have led him to fear that, if he crossed his father, it would damage him, such as by causing a heart attack. He needed to see his father regularly to be sure he was all right, not damaged by his, the son's, impulses to separate from his father's dominion.

Meanwhile, Esther was becoming disillusioned with her romantic notion that her husband would do anything for her. Some part of his loyalty was still firmly attached to his parents and probably always would be. She did not want to be like her mother-in-law, whom she saw as a compliant wife with no real voice in family matters. She could not, however, barrage her husband with these thoughts. He would just feel criticized and defensive, and close himself off from her. She needed to use strategies such as praising him for being a loyal son— use a compliment in place of a criticism. This would have the paradoxical effect of getting him to think about what was keeping him so loyal. She could also ask him questions that would slowly expand his perspective, such as what kind of father had his grandfather been? It is likely that a cross-generational pattern of selfishness would emerge. As a therapist, Esther could follow through on these recommendations.

An excellent metaphor for intimacy is the one about porcupines. When porcupines get close they poke each other, so they pull away.

When they withdraw, they get cold and lonely, so they snuggle up again. It brings an association to the old nursery rhyme, "Needles and pins, Needles and pins/When a man marries, his trouble begins." A noted psychotherapist, Leslie Rosenthal, jibes that a marriage is not a real marriage unless each member of the couple contemplates divorce at least once a month, if not every day.

True love? Psychotherapist Hattie Rosenthal has exhorted, "If you can't get the whole loaf, get all the crumbs you can." What I notice is that, fulfilling our needs for love—which are experienced sometimes as a need for connectedness, sometimes for support, sometimes as an outlet for our bad temper, sometimes for a sense of identity, sometimes for mentoring, sometimes for a sexual partner, sometimes for a play-mate—takes a lot of people and a lot of time. Those on whom we depend may include our spouse, our parents, our children and their families, our old friends, our current mentors, our colleagues, the professional or social groups with which we are affiliated, our clients, our exercise buddies, our coterie of friends who share cultural interests, our protégées, our siblings, our exercise coaches, our computer technicians, and our pets, to name a few. No one relationship could provide what this crowd does.

H. LOVE, OPTIMISM, AND THE SENIOR CITIZEN

A problem with intimacy is that a great deal of tension is aroused simply by the frustrations of daily living. Our mounting destructive impulses create the need for a release. How do we keep from inflicting our frustration onto the most convenient target (our spouse) and instead give off the kinds of positive feelings that will keep our partner alive and at our side? Erik Erikson noted that people with emotional maturity recognize this in one another. They share the final stage in emotional growth, which he called "integrity." By this, he meant being able to integrate their feelings, as evidenced by their not inflicting them on others. True maturity entails accepting everything about being human.

In the quiet myth of Baucis and Philemon, the Greeks portrayed the integrity of an elderly couple. Though they barely had enough food to feed themselves, they nonetheless managed to be hospitable to strangers, as per the tradition of their culture. On one occasion the visitors who knocked at their door turned out to be the gods Jupiter and Mercury in disguise. These two had been turned away at every other door they approached and were grateful when, at last, they were welcomed in to share the humble meal and lodging offered by the elderly pair. In thanks, the gods granted them one wish. After conferring together, the couple requested that neither of them should outlive the other. When their time came, this wish was granted, and the two were simultaneously turned into an oak and a linden tree intertwined so as to form one trunk, their leaves forever whispering together.

Several elements in this story are striking: the attitude of optimism and resourcefulness of the couple, the gods whom they entertain, and their being granted a sort of immortality as separate species of trees. Optimism, and a sense of control over one's destiny, are strongly correlated with physical health and longevity. Even Louis Pasteur, discoverer of the role of microbes in illness, acknowledged on his deathbed, *"Le germ n'est rien, c'est le terrain qui est tout"* (The germ is nothing, it's the host that is everything.) The human immune system can handle pathogens, if only it will. Hans Selye, the renowned pioneer in stress research, similarly found that it is not adverse stimuli that damage us, but our attitude toward them. He, too, recommended finding a way to stay optimistic.

At their death, Baucis and Philemon are transformed into *separate kinds* of trees. This detail suggests that individuation is a key to lengthy relationships and longevity. This is in opposition to enmeshment, where each partner is expected to live within the confines of an assigned identity. Oaks and lindens, like most trees, live far longer than the human life span. This detail offers the reassurance of extending intimacy forever, quelling anxiety about one predeceasing the other. The immortality of nature indeed is without end. Environmentalists recognize the contribution that senescent and dead trees make as a habitat for many species of life. We, too, can neutralize our experience of the many losses we suffer as we age by knowing that, like trees, we will be together forever, through all the time of existence and beyond. For when we die, we dissolve and our dust intermingles with the elements of all of nature. To paraphrase the poet Rupert Brooke, we leave a richer dust on earth for our having lived there.

Intimacy with the self (self-love) results from an ability to learn from our experiences with others. Wisdom is achieved when we cease expecting ourselves or others to be different from, or better than, we/they are. It requires the realization that there is no such thing as the unconditional love for which the infant within us forever yearns. It requires giving up expecting everything from any one relationship. It requires making friends with our unconscious—the little child inside us with its boundless wishes and disappointments.

On a more difficult plane, maturity and wisdom require the ability to sacrifice others sooner than sacrifice ourselves. This means not fretting so much about others' feelings. Ultimately each person is responsible for his or her own—no one can make us happy but we ourselves. It also necessitates being comfortable with loving and hating the same person—not a problem so long as we continue to act in a friendly way.

It means learning to live with the behavior of our loved ones as they are, not pressuring them to become our narcissistic twins or ideals. It means realizing we will never get all our emotional needs met by any one person, and so we should enjoy whatever crumbs we find wherever we find them. Simply said, for most of us the advantages of having a life partner outweigh the disadvantages. On balance, life is easier two by two.

Outside of myself, my most intimate relationship is my marriage. It gives me security and stability. I spoon my stomach against my husband's warm backside in the dark of night when I feel restless and full of angst, and I feel as though his flesh absorbs my tension. I have contemplated divorce or separation over the years, basically with the fantasy that I could get an even better life. It was not that my own was intolerable, but the thought that someone out there could magically relieve me of every last shred of misery. I observed my peers breaking up, so why shouldn't I? I think unconsciously the partner I most wanted was my father.

Fortunately, I was at first too insecure to take the risk of divorce, and later too aware of the fact that no one but I myself could alleviate my discontent. There were periods in my life when I withdrew from my husband, as earlier I had withdrawn from my mother, with the same punishing intent. In my psychotherapy I have made the connection that my anger at my husband most often results from my unconscious projection onto him of traits I hated about my mother and traits I hate about myself. Since my husband is a quiet man who does not talk much about his feelings, I am left with my fantasies of what they might be if he spoke them. For a depressive, the fantasy is always worse than reality. Also, like my mother before me, who hated both her husbands for not realizing her ambitions (or were they *her* mother's?), I hated my husband for what I perceived as his deficiencies, another thing I hated about myself. Yet how could I leave a man for traits I myself possessed?

I have always known my husband to be honest and kind and someone I could rely upon. He provides romance as well as excellent problem-solving skills. Our genes, and our future, are forever commingled in our children. Even so, our many differences create animosity in our daily life. For example, he loves to listen to music played at full volume when he is working around the house. I can't stand the noise. It interferes with my wish to drift along in my own thoughts. I am comfortable asking him to lower the volume. He can't understand why I don't appreciate the way music is best when it crashes like a thunderstorm. We disappoint one another in this and many other ways. We each have many needs we cannot realize for one another.

It was once both frightening and painful for me not to try to fulfill him in every way. I felt that was my duty as a wife, though I no longer do. The only one who can fulfill him is he himself. My job of fulfilling myself is enough of a task for any human being. Now that we both seem to have agreed about this, we are discovering we can enjoy one another's company regardless. We marvel at how differently we react. Developing the ability to observe ourselves, we become able to laugh at ourselves as if we were the players in some absurd sit-com.

I have chafed at the idea that I must consult my husband about my plans, if only to keep the peace. It felt as if I was not free to choose spontaneously. Consciously, I know that marital intimacy requires compromise and sacrifice, and my anxieties compelled me to be submissive. At the same time, my frisky impulses urged me to be selfish. There is no easy solution to this dilemma. I feel it is important to be safe, but it is also important to provide satisfactions for myself. The dangerous ones, to have affairs or spend money on superficial indulgences, I pander to in small ways. I flirt with, or fantasize about, attractive men; I go shopping; I go to my chiropractor, who is not only brilliant at banishing any ache or pain, but is handsome as the devil as well. Furthermore, I remain in therapy, which in effect means paying someone to pay attention to me.

There used to be times when I projected onto my husband the idea that he disapproved of me. I read his facial expression to find confirmation of this as fact. When I started *asking* him instead of making self-fulfilling assumptions, I discovered that he is far more accepting than I had ever imagined. He is even a little intimidated by me. Well, that is a fun thought.

An example of the way old dramas from my past manifest in my day-to-day marital life occurred when we rented a house for a week's summer vacation. I obsessively scrubbed and vacuumed on the last day, leaving the place cleaner than it had been on our arrival. My husband couldn't see the need to do this and barely pitched in. I threw a little tantrum when he thoughtlessly obstructed one step of my housekeeping. For a moment I felt pure hatred for him, and had a fierce wish to be free of him once and for all. As I have learned to do, I exhaled deeply a couple of times and then gave myself the kind of self-talk I have learned in my therapy. I recognized that my compulsive cleaning replicated the way my mother had behaved in my childhood when we moved out of one home and into another. Maniacally cleaning, as my mother had done long ago, gave me feelings of closeness with her. As my mother often had, I'd blown a fuse over a trivial piece of nonsense. But where once I would have called myself stupid and inadequate for putting on such a scene, I just observed myself being difficult. Finding the source in my early emotional experience, I accepted and forgave myself, and this helped me recover from my bad humor. I also gave myself permission to ask my husband to apologize, and he tolerantly complied. Once upon a time he would have been too attached to being right to abide by my request for an apology. And as I thought about it, I admired myself for leaving the house so clean. I imagined the owner's pleasure on opening the door to the gleam and tidiness of her house, even as I would feel pleasure if someone did the same for me. Yes, I recognized myself as neurotic. I am familiar with the phenomenon of "housewife's psychosis," wherein women make family members miserable with their obsessive cleaning. I knew I was erring in that direction, but I also felt compassion toward the little child in me who loves and wants to be like her mother, unreasonable though she was.

Talking together as a couple is difficult. Our parents' generation encouraged children to listen, not talk. Also, as children of the culture of the Great Depression, we each learned not to ask for things, not to be selfish or greedy. When we were first married I played along with the fiction that I thought he was perfect. Actually, I needed to see him as wiser and more knowledgeable than I to help me finish growing up. Sex was a wonderful distraction for us both to avoid seeing how infantile we were, stumbling along pretending that we knew how to cope.

My husband's and my sexual excitement with one another, an important basis for our early intimacy as well as an outlet for our tensions, has subsided over the years. My mother modeled her obvious enjoyment of sex and of getting men aroused, so again this aspect of me is a form of intimacy with her, to my husband's benefit. The secret thrill of our sex life has been somewhat replaced by the challenge of our learning to communicate in other ways. As a young woman I was submissive and undemanding, but now I have become assertive. I think he finds it stimulating, because he is becoming more conversationally active as well, and I appreciate it. Enough of the strong silent type! My current belief is that we can each help the other get what they want so that neither of us has to sacrifice. Both of us can win. We have learned to encourage one another to pursue our separate interests, to spend money on ourselves in indulgent ways, and most of all to speak up.

The great British psychotherapist D.W. Winnicott uses the word "muddle" to depict how we get through ordinary life. I see myself as a late middle-aged woman muddling along in a mostly successful way. "Muddle" is a cozy word with childlike undertones, suggesting the awkwardness we experience groping with the conundrums of our existence. I believe I have mostly matured from being a passive child-wife who yearned for a magical happy ending of some sort, into a mostly successful adult professional and marital partner mostly realizing there are no happy endings, but resolving to have as good a time as I can anyway.

I. AWARENESS OF DEATH'S APPROACH

I am at an age when I can no longer avoid thinking about death, my own or that of my same aged relatives and friends. Most people my age have already lost their parents and are now starting to lose friends and family closer to themselves in age. Mourning is painful and exhausting. My two best friends and I meet together and discuss what is going on inside us when we have occasion to grieve—the darkness, the hopelessness, the pain and sorrow, and then the surprising moments as we start to recover. I recently told them my favorite memory of my father, which was the way he would cry when we met after a separation of a year or two, fat tears splashing onto the airport's concrete floor as I ran to meet him. "I'm putting that memory in my pocket," exclaimed my friend Barbara. It made me appreciate my treasured memory all the more, so I told some others. I remembered the time my daddy took my sister, my stepbrother, and me hiking in Waimea Canyon on his home island of Kauai. The trail rose high over a ridge and then descended deeply into the rainforest valley, the wettest place on earth. Trudging back up the steep slope on our way home, I became exhausted and weepy, so my dad swung me up onto his powerful shoulders and carried me out. Afterwards, he would tenderly refer to that adventure as "the pooped-out bosky dell." Yet another time he took us rowing inside the big reef that faced his beach home at Haena. We each had a hand line with a baited hook. First my sister and then my brother caught a fine fish, but I had no luck. My daddy took my hand line and dove with it into the ocean where he disappeared under the shelf of the reef for a while. When he came back up I had a nice fat fish on my line, too.

CHAPTER 11

PRACTICING GOOD EMOTIONAL HYGEINE

A. Conversations Among My Many Selves

PHYSICAL HYGIENE IS TAUGHT in health classes at school. Why not teach emotional hygiene as well? I find that working on my self-esteem is a daily necessity, equivalent to showering, exercising, and limiting my intake of sweets. The same way my immune system deals with dangers in my body, my mind has to manage the thoughts, feelings, and impulses that might otherwise derail me. I view this as taking care of my mental hygiene, and give myself "sessions" in which I dose myself with understanding and self-acceptance.

A clever person in my field once described this as repairing our IALAC ("I Am Lovable and Capable") badge. I am usually the first one to take bites out of my own. "Why aren't I as clever, wise, funny, pretty, youthful, rich, tough, talented, fortunate, athletic, disciplined, smart—you name it—as that person over there?" As I condemn myself, my self-esteem shrivels, but then other selves in my mind pull me back up from despair.

Here are the sorts of things I say to myself to repair my IALAC badge:

"Hey! Don't I have the prettiest garden on my block?"

"Big deal," attacks my inner demon self. "You live on a very short block."

My healthy "I" defends me: "But I get nice compliments from dog walkers and baby carriage pushers. They stop and take the time to do that."

Demon: "Great." (said witheringly—my mother's voice.) "It doesn't take talent to make a garden, just dirty, hard work."

Healthy "I" (claws exposed): "Wait a minute! I *chose* the things that are growing there. I have flowers blooming continuously from March through October. That is an accomplishment."

In my self-sessions I review the causes for my tendency to fall into depression. Yes, some of it is undoubtedly genetic—my austere Nordic genes. Not much I can do about them. Let them have their moment and move on. More workable are my hurtful memories about my mother. She divorced my father, a very loving guy, when I was four, took me five thousand miles away, dumped me in a boarding school, and disappeared. Six interminable months later she sent me back to live with my father for a year. I learned to survive without her, but at the cost of having a bruised and frightened heart. My inner conversation from then on consisted of exchanges between a forlorn little girl self and my relentlessly disapproving, falsely capable demon self. The demon kept me together, but at the price of self-condemnation. My therapist self understands this, and is forgiving.

My therapist self adds a benevolent presence to my internal conversation. After many years of undergoing my own therapy, it has become part of me. Simply put, this means I have memories of my relationship with my actual therapist and of how he helps me see myself in compassionate ways. My therapist self mirrors my actual therapist, and so is reasonable and kind, very experienced and sure of nerself. When my demon self sneers about my worthlessness, my therapist self demurs: "Listen! It is perfectly understandable that I feel worthless sometimes, given the painful traumas of my early childhood." My therapist self can bring in reinforcements: "Nobel Laureates in neuroscience have confirmed what Freud observed about the unconscious nature of the mind and the lingering effect of traumatic memories. So back off, demon self!"

Encouraging me to feel furious, which makes me feel powerful and back on top of the world, my therapist self reasons, "How could I not be self-attacking? That bitch my mother couldn't wait to get rid of me. And then she turned me into her slave." (With the demon self's help, back then, my mother got me to bury my own needs and always say, "Yes, mother dear," to hers.)

My ability to feel anger and use its energy to fight my demon self is essential to my mental hygiene. Before my therapy, any expression of anger frightened me, even my own. The forlorn little girl part of my mind believed that having an angry thought meant I was unfit for human society and really belonged in lonely isolation at a boarding school/ prison. With her belief in wish and magic, my forlorn little girl self assumed I could harm someone just by harboring a momentary hateful thought. But my therapist self chuckles: "Yeah, yeah, yeah. If wishes could kill, that would be the end of human life on this planet." Knowing that depression is essentially a habit of turning my anger against myself, my therapist self urges me to turn it back outward onto others (only in feeling, not in deed)—especially onto my mother (who is long dead).

My awareness that anger is a healthy, normal feeling makes me feel at ease with it. Instead of feeling stricken when someone roars at me (or I roar at myself for being foolish), I draw back into silent reflection. I think about how it can be healthful for that person to blow off some steam. Yes, sometimes I have an impulse to punish the person if he or she frightens me, but then my rational self reasons, "What does punishment ever accomplish other than to set off endless cycles of retaliation? Do I want to spend my time and energy doing that? No!" My therapist self knows that my former panic about anger resulted from terror of my mother that got stuck in my emotional memory bank when I was a four-year-old in boarding school. I assumed I had caused her to abandon me. That is the way a child's mind works—blaming itself when a parent hurts it. So it is restorative to remind myself of this as well.

Some injuries to my IALAC badge result from my narcissistic need to be around others who act like me and who agree with me. Sometimes some of my colleagues seem not to, and this leads me to suffer self-doubt. Some colleagues are more fashion-conscious than I, for example, and comport themselves as consummate professionals, whereas I tend to be artistic, creative, and impulsive. I particularly like being silly. Occasionally I feel my colleagues think I am worthless, and would just as soon that I disappear. My paranoid self! But then an assertive self comes forward and says, "What the hell! You ain't bad, kid! I like you just fine!" Others of my colleagues are fun-loving creatives like me, and around them I don't feel so eccentric. I need my reasonable adult self to remind me that everyone's competencies are needed. My adult self knows that my narcissism, like everyone else's, is just another human dilemma that must be accommodated because it can never be resolved.

I am an advocate of using four-letter words as the fastest and most satisfying way of dealing with anger. They are equally suitable for telling off a rude driver (from the safety of my locked car, windows up) or the rock against which I stub my toe. Some "dirty words" come from my toilet training stage, others from my Oedipal stage. The fact that using them was a punishable act in childhood adds the magic potency of for-biddenness! Without that cheek, the magic would deflate.

My therapist self, cruising about in my neocortex, can be slow on the uptake compared to the jaguar speed of my demon self lurking in my emotional brain. My demon self is valuable for its instant re-action times to danger. But my therapist self, high up in my brain's attic, has the knowledge base and the more relaxed timing required to figure out the big picture. This is comforting. In contrast to the way I was raised, when the loudest, most furious voice (my mother's) held all the power, the voice of reason (my therapist self) speaks cooly, softly. It is hard to hear until my clamoring emotions cool down. I honor and cultivate my soft voice. It helps me challenge the thunderous demands for attention—screaming headlines, high-deci-bel advertisements, scheming Machiavellian politicians—that seem to permeate our world. If something is not at the extreme end of su-perlative, it's just wallpaper until my therapist self comments, "Baloney!"

My therapist self combines with other adult selves in my head: the rational self, the skilled teacher, the doting grandmother, the contented wife. These voices agree that I have some accomplishments under my belt. They also harbor sweet memories to neutralize my blues. I keep handy a poem written by an inner-city high school student who had been in my writing class for a year:

SHEILA
(Written by AIRBORNE, aka Anguished Novice, May 7, 1985)

Sealed up like a tomb,
Focusing in on people like a radar disc,

Covering your young with love in an unnoticeable way,
You're like a dragon in the middle of a hurricane,
Fierce but at the same time gentle—
Like an eagle, you scope in on your prey.
You make simple ideas so profound and mysterious,
Sheila. . .
You build a gate of thorns around your thoughts,
Like a chameleon, you can adjust to anyone instantly.
In your own clever way
You are as unpredictable as the weather,
You're one mysterious treasure chest. . .
Sheila. . .

This student, the same as many others, was floored by my ability to stay calm in the face of their excitability, "like a dragon in. . .a hurricane. . ." It made me powerful in their eyes. And what natural poets they were, as teenagers with their untamed passions always are.

My English-teacher self finds solace in literature that shows how writers I admire have similarly suffered from painful moments. The American poet, Emily Dickinson, for example:

42

I'm nobody. Who are you?
Are you nobody too?
Then there's a pair of us.
Don't tell—they'd banish us, you know.

How dreary to be somebody,

How public—like a frog—
To tell your name the livelong June
To an admiring bog.

Dickenson was a recluse who almost never left her parents' home. My impression is that in the second stanza she is trying to convince herself that her isolation from the world was something positive. I'm glad that, unlike her, I escaped.

Like most great writers, Shakespeare was no stranger to depression:

Sonnet XXIX

When in disgrace with fortune and men's eyes
I all alone beweep my outcast state,
And trouble deaf heaven with my bootless cries,
And look upon myself, and curse my fate,
Wishing me like to one more rich in hope,
Featured like him, like him with friends possessed,
Desiring this man's art, and that man's scope,
With what I most enjoy contented least;
Yet in these thoughts my self almost despising,
Haply I think on thee, and then my state,
Like to the lark at break of day arising
From sullen earth, sings hymns at heaven's gate;
For thy sweet love remembered such wealth brings
That then I scorn to change my state with kings.

Aside from the brilliance with which he expresses what I struggle to say, what I love in this sonnet is that Shakespeare heals himself by thinking of his loved one: "For thy sweet love remembered such wealth brings/ That then I scorn to change my state with kings." He knew the psychological truth that it is our relationships that inspire us to recover from depression and to live well.

Clearly, I need many ways to battle my demon self, who will never stop popping up with comments like "Your life has been worthless. You might as well be dead." As I advance in years, my aging crone self has a healing daydream of someone saying something nice at my funeral. Here is my doting grandmother fantasy of how my six-year-old granddaughter might eulogize me:

"We had so much fun at my Grammy's house. We put on karate shows. Grammy fed us our favorite food— steamed edamame beans that we squeezed into our mouths—and she made us tea parties with humongous rainbow fruit platters for snack." Just thinking of giving my grandchildren pleasure makes my heart sing.

Knowledge offered by the deeply experienced, professional part of my therapist self is a resource without bounds. For example, I know that, when other people mistreat me or, in some uncanny way, get me to feel miserable about myself, it is because they "induce" that feeling in me. To maintain their self-esteem, they provoke in me a painful feeling they do not want to feel themselves—inferiority, helplessness, guilt, shame, or the like. Observing that other person over time, and seeing how he or she does the same thing with others, my knowing this always gets confirmed. It makes it possible for me to understand the other person and at the same time have a therapeutic thought about myself. It also helps me be aware of what motivated the horrid tyrants of history—the mass murderers, those who lacked all human empathy, etc. Inside they, too, suffered, as they made others suffer.

When my analytic colleagues trip up and berate me with angry words or an angry voice, I let them know it: "I want you to speak to me in a friendly way regardless of what you feel," I say.

One colleague countered, "But I'm *angry* at you!"

"I *still* want you to talk to me in a nice way," I insisted, reminding her about what we therapists always preach: "Maturity consists of having all our feelings but still acting appropriately—meaning in a friendly and constructive way."

My colleague came to her senses: "You're right. Just remind me when I'm a bitch." So I do.

My interior conversation among all these selves never ends. Emotional safety can only come from nurturing these different aspects of my mind, each with its unique voice, wisdom, and power. Having them inside counters and detoxifies the endless flow of my daily frustrations, disappointments, and tragedies, and the feelings they stimulate, feelings that could otherwise lay me low.

B. CONNECTING THE DOTS
BETWEEN STRESS AND ILLNESS

The great stress researcher Hans Selye discovered that it is our emotional overreaction to stimulation that causes our adrenal glands to flood our system with cortisol. The destructive effect of this hormone cascade on our health is well established. Most health problems are caused or worsened by cortisol-induced inflammation—from arthritis to autoimmune illness, to heart disease, to emotional disorders. Add to this the current recognition that alexithymia, the inability to know or report what one is feeling, can be a contributing factor to major illnesses. Without words to describe our emotions, communication with others and ourselves is blocked. Our body/mind is then more vulnerable to fluctuations in internal or external pressure. Blockage in any living system is detrimental to life. How important it is to talk about everything!

As a psychotherapist, I focus on the way our unconscious makes use of symbols and metaphors to express itself, but how does this transfer to the workings of our body? We know now that there is a division of labor between the brain's left and right hemispheres. With its language center, our left hemisphere is the locus of our systematic, cognitive problem solving. Perhaps for this reason it is by nature optimistic. Our right hemisphere, however, is silent, pessimistic, visual, creative, poetic (using symbols and metaphors), and, I think, playful. Right hemisphere processing (along with the intertwining of the emotional and cognitive centers of the midbrain and frontal cortex) is central to what we call the unconscious.

Other important aspects of brain process and structure contribute to what we experience as the unconscious aspects of our mind. Joseph LeDoux (1998, 2002) has shown that the emotional centers of the brain, when excited, shut down the prefrontal cortex where our judgment, empathy, and perspective reside. As the interaction of our cognition and emotion comes to a halt, the mind loses its rational balance.

The amygdalas, small structures located in the midbrain, make sure that we learn the lessons of our terrifying experiences. Trauma researchers like Lenore Terr note that harrowing memories can have extraordinary and lasting clarity, searing the mind with the sights, sounds, smells, and emotions surrounding an event. Trauma victims have vivid flashbacks of these data. The treatment Terr recommends is for victims to talk together. Mutual talk helps them regain a sense of control over their own fate. Inseparability of the mind and the body means both physical and emotional health are at risk when there is overload or blockage. Strangulated affect can erupt in pathological symptoms.

C. Killing My Mother

A few weeks after the death of my mother, a swollen, crimson knot appeared on my neck. For a while it went unnoticed as I wept and grieved. Guilt flooded through me day and night. It was I who killed her. No getting around it. Having my neck and shoulder frozen in pain seemed trivial next to my wracking guilt.

My mother had known "the big one" was coming. Her heart had been fibrillating continuously for several years, pooling blood in the bottom of one ventricle so that clots formed. It gave her frequent TIAs—transient ischemic attacks (small strokes)—that she seemed to brush off as of no great moment. She was always one to deny strong feelings. She never looked ill. Her dancer's posture and slender waist maintained the illusion of her athletic youth. Except, when I saw her some months before her final devastating stroke, I was startled to see her ride to her departure gate at the airport in a wheelchair. With a little spurt of alarm in my chest, I wondered if it could be true. Was she really approaching her final decline? How does hope blend with pain and rage, for that is what I felt? Ours had always been a troubled relationship.

She had told everyone—my stepfather (sweet man, he objects to the "step" and never uses it, so I won't either), my siblings, her doctor—that when, not if, the big stroke came, she did not want to be kept alive by machine.

I doubt any of us could wrap our minds around the implications of her request. "Yes, yes," we promised, turning our thoughts elsewhere. Her weekly letters continued to arrive on schedule with news of the family and her social life. She maintained the illusion that everything was going along as it always had and always would.

And then the phone call: "Your mother's had a stroke. It looks bad, but the doctors are still doing tests. They're just not sure of the extent of the damage, and of what kind of rehabilitation might be possible. Perhaps you should come home."

Remembering this moment, I am back there again. My heart thuds as my thoughts eddy from denial to dread to, yes, relief. At last! My fear of her will end! No more of her haunting disapproval. And— I might finally get something from her while I am still young enough to enjoy it. But my god, how can I gloat at a time like this? "How bad?" I query.

"She can't even swallow," my father responds, his breath raspy with sorrow.

I fly the six thousand miles home to Maui, apprehensive, sad, angry, and numb. What will it be like to see my mother lying helpless and inert?

My three siblings and I assemble at my parents' mountain home and then set out with my father on the long drive down mountain to the nursing facility in Kahului where my mother lies on an airbed in her second floor room. She is propped so as to have a view up the slopes of the mountains of West Maui, a vista of paradise in all its ordinary green and sunny splendor.

She is awake. To my relief she looks just like herself, beautiful and of course serene—no trace of the frown that could mar her brow. Standing at her side I make eye contact with her, and immediately well with tears—of grief, of shame, of anger, of victory. "Mom, I love you. I'm so sorry about this." I step away wringing my hands.

Later, I hear my father whisper to her, "Ginger, don't leave me."

Her neurologist gives us his report. There is no hope of any kind of recovery. Since she cannot even scroll her eyes up and down, or blink to signal "yes" or "no," she is locked in. She does not meet the minimum standard for rehabilitation, which would be an ability to establish some form of communication.

We meet with her personal physician in a little waiting room down the hall. "Yes," he grants, "she told me not to keep her alive artificially. The problem is there is no way to tell if she has changed her mind. So I cannot recommend removal of life support. I can probably keep her alive for another year."

Huddling in the hallway my sister, my brothers, my father, and I poll one another. "We promised her," my sister implores. One by one we nod in agreement. But then we retreat into the privacy of our inner thoughts. As a family we do not talk about feelings.

We call a local hospice program that sends over someone to counsel us. "You would be doing what she wished," she soothes. "No, she is not in pain. You are doing the right thing." She hands us each a pamphlet informing us of what to expect in the coming days.

We tell the doctor to "pull the plug." He accedes but then scolds, "She is going to suffer from dehydration. At least you should let her have an I.V." He stomps off in a huff. My head reels with the implication of his words. I have not given consideration to the idea that she might suffer, but how could she not? I cannot open my mouth to say anything. I feel weak, belly-punched. I am grateful for his care. I am furious at his provocative tone, his refusal to share the burden of decision.

That evening, back up the mountain, my sister and I open the secret drawer where mother keeps her jewelry. Inside there is a handwritten list of each item designating who is to get what. I am thrilled to learn I am to get a diamond ring that once belonged to my great aunt. It is clearly a valuable piece of jewelry, more expensive than anything I have ever owned. Telling myself it is for safekeeping, I put it on my finger and admire it there. But the next day at mother's bedside I remember that she can still see. Does she see me marveling at the ring on my finger? What am I doing flaunting possession of something she undoubtedly prizes right there in front of her? How insulting to act as if she is already gone.

Life support is removed, but my mother lingers day after day. The massive dose of antibiotics she has been given wards off the pneumonia the doctor says will take her. Without a swallowing reflex, her saliva slides into her lungs. She is inert, but when I look into her eyes, there she is.

Each morning we arrive in her room, and she appears the same— bright, clean, lovely. We sense, or perhaps project, that she is glad to see us, that she enjoys being the center of our attention. We take turns standing by her head and fussing over her, talking to her. My father solves his daily crossword puzzle, speaking the clues and his solutions in her ears. My sister-in-law paints my mother's toenails pearl pink, holding up each foot for her to see how pretty. From time to time my mother's close friends come by, telling her the jokes and gossip she always loved. "*Tashi bobo!* Ginger," greets her childhood girlfriend in a bright twitter.

The elderly Japanese woman in the next bed squawks, "*Hanh?*" In her language it is as foul an insult as one can express. We giggle into our hands.

Waiting is agony. I keep wondering, Is she thirsty? Is she suffering? Is she feeling things behind her expressionless face? She can't even squint or shed a tear in pain or sadness. The doctor says the stroke destroyed her cerebellum, which explains her total paralysis. But he says she is conscious, she can listen and think. What does that mean, *conscious*? Can she really think? What is she thinking? Can she feel without a body to tense up with emotion? What is it like having her family fulfill her request to kill her?

Her nurses tenderly bathe her, but on the sixth day there is a smell like an old kitchen sponge. Her skin feels slick and crumbly, as if gone to mold. I can't look at her. I take a long walk around the neighborhood. I have nothing to say to her. I have everything to say to her. Shall I finally tell her how much she hurt me? Bring on another stroke—finish her off? I cringe in horror. I feel so alone. My brothers have gone back to their lives. Only my sister, my father, and I keep the vigil. We talk about arrangements as if our inner turmoil doesn't exist.

On the eighth day mother begins turning blue. It starts at her toes and slowly moves up, so we know the end is at hand. Her fever soars to 108 degrees. She seems to be breathing with her shoulders, and her eyes have lost their focus. My sister notices that the lens implants from her cataract surgery have hemorrhaged to the surface of her corneas.

I numbly roam the silent corridor. Towards noon, my sister calls for me to come quick. She, my father, and I witness the grotesque paroxysm that signals mother's end. It is over.

We go back up the mountain, speaking haltingly about a memorial service. Things are left undecided. I remember nothing further until I am home in flatland New Jersey, steeped in gloom. I keep reflecting about how, since my biological father is dead, I am now an orphan, on the front lines of death myself. No one is left to buffer me from thoughts of my mortality. My mind shifts to my relief that there is no one left on the globe who can hurt me as my mother had. I will never fear anyone as I feared her. I drift to thoughts of my inheritance. How shall I spend it? I twist my glittering ring and my mood swings back again to guilt. I have committed murder.

I mention the knot on my neck in my therapy. I speak about my horror, my guilt, my victory—I have outlived her! And my hate. I hate her for her miserliness with me in life. I hate her for abandoning me as a small girl. I hate her for the things I am not—not as pretty as she, not as fine an athlete, not as sheltered. I hate her for never acknowledging my accomplishments. I hate her because I never could speak my mind to her. I hate her for never having grown up. I hate myself. I killed her. I always wanted to kill her. I am a murderess. My neck hurts. I finger the lump throbbing below my ear. It feels hotter, swelling above the collar of my turtleneck sweater.

At some pause in my flow of talk, my therapist asks, in his soft, comforting voice,

"Is that the knot on the noose with which you have hanged yourself?"

I lie in stunned silence.

"Of course. Yes, that's what it is," I finally say. I weep softly as my tension begins to drain. Ah, the relief. Within hours the knot diminishes to almost nothing, and the next day it is as if it had never been.

D. DECONSTRUCTING THE LUMP ON MY NECK

Why and how did my painful symptom arise, and what enabled its eventual release? What theoretical map led my therapist to his merciful intervention? Theoretical conjecture is most exciting when it is the solution to a living puzzle. Here is my attempt.

The mind and body are a continuum, each an extension of the other. Not just the cells in our brain, but each cell in our body has memories. There are receptors for the brain's transmitting substances on them all. Whatever we feel affects us from head to toe, including the cells of our immune system. All our feelings coexist in this continuum. Our murderous feelings are an extension of our loving feelings, and vice versa. Conflict about our ambivalence is only an artifact of our using words to separate our feelings. In nature there is no such split. Life is an energy stream dependent on continuous feedback loops of conscious and unconscious processing, of communication with our environment and within our body. Problems arise when some force cuts off or short-circuits this sweeping flow.

By joining in my family's decision to withhold life support, I killed my mother. On top of my painful ambivalence at losing her and my distress from the deathbed vigil, my terrible guilt engulfed me. Since my family's ethos prohibits discussion about feelings, being with them isolated me from the potential of soothing discharge through conversation. Instead, my troubled thoughts and emotions were bottled up in my sensorium.

I speculate that an excess of brain hormones—those conveying guilt, sorrow, loss, anguish of every sort—caromed through my body, seeking release. The emotional centers of my brain signaled "emergency!" to my adrenal glands. Cortisol tightened the muscles of my back, shoulders, and neck, preparing them for fight or flight, pinching off their natural flow. My brain's right hemisphere, wordless but creative, contributed a metaphor to bind my enormous guilt—the symbolic knot on the hangman's noose. Cleverly, it managed to encapsulate guilt, punishment, self-hatred, anger (the redness), and sorrow (the pain) in its creation.

My therapist's intervention was based on his understanding of how the unconscious finds expression through symbols and metaphors. Hearing my extreme self-reproach, he put two plus two together, intuiting the meaning of the knot. He enabled me to talk and think about it, thus creating an outlet to drain my tension. His listening and understanding absorbed my stress and allowed my optimistic, logical, articulate, left hemisphere self to return to the fore. I could once more eng____ in reassuring self-talk: "I am only human. Humans have not evolved sufficiently to cope with the kind of ethical dilemma I confronted on that grim day when my family convened in the hospital. In the days of my ancestors, my mother would have died at home swiftly and mercifully of pneumonia, what they used to call 'the old person's friend.'"

Back home in Hawaii with my family, I had been locked into silence, as paralyzed as my mother was, for all that I had an intact brain. I fell into the regression most people experience on a visit home. The traumatic nature of my visit, and my family's characteristic muzzle of silence, were further aggravations. That my feelings became trapped under the circumstances is natural and understandable.

Yes, I am a killer, but ordinarily I would not have acted out this totally human potential. If I had not voted to remove life support, I would have broken a promise to my mother. I would also have isolated myself from the remainder of my tribe—my sister, brothers, and father. My guilt began long before her illness. I had felt murderous anger towards her since I was a little girl, but not without reason. I had been both a good daughter and a terrible daughter, as my mother had been both a good and a terrible mother. Yet wishes do not kill, however much the small child lingering in my unconscious believes they may.

I am reassured as I attempt to explain the mysteries of the brain. It relieves my terror of the unknown and protects me from the condemnatory mores by which I was raised. My family's way of managing emotions had always been to treat them as something that should properly be kept to oneself. Any expression of distress or anger was considered self-indulgent. Their implied belief is that, when you smother a feeling, it fades and disappears. Shaming was their most potent tool: "Don't be a baby!"

As a therapist I have learned there is no such thing as an evil thought or feeling. Actions can cause damage, but feelings are just data, albeit sometimes scary data. When I am able to give my feelings consideration, to talk about them with the people I trust, they are not a problem, not even my destructive ones.

Flowing freely, the human mind is fundamentally ambivalent. We think one thing and then its reverse. We no sooner feel one emotion than we flit to its polar opposite. This keeps us in balance. The communication systems of our mind/body are meant to stream with life in all its contradictions. Except for the narrow window of our current focus, what neuroscientists call "working memory," most of this goes on outside of our awareness. What we experience as consciousness is only a tiny tip of the iceberg of our thinking.

As a theorist, I fantasize myself as unconsciously poised on a balance beam between impulses to live and impulses to die. My interests and connections inspire me towards the living side, and my frustrations and terrors toward the death side. To maintain my balance I try to think it all, to feel it all, to say it all, the symphony of my existence. Did I kill my mother? Yes. And no. I asked the doctor to pull the plug, but I did not cause her to have her massive stroke. Would I do it again? I hope I am never called upon to do so, because I don't think I could. In part this is because the burden of guilt was so painful, but also because I am not sure I would want it done to me. I think I might want to stay alive purely out of curiosity—there is so much yet to see and learn and hear and think. I recognize my answer is skewed by my current state of good health. Scientists now recognize there is no ultimate truth, just the best explanation for what has been observed until a better one comes along. Here I have given the best that I can come up with, given what I know at this time.

CHAPTER 12

MASTERING
THE WORLD
OF EMOTIONS

A. ANTICIPATING CHALLENGES

WHAT IS THE BEST way for a family to educate its children emotionally? Since everything about us is unique, this presents a real challenge. It is the family's job to help each child discover what is right and meaningful for them. Whether it is food, sleep schedules, learning styles, pastimes, or playmates, each child is the only living expert on the best choices for himself or herself. The problem is, parents are not taught this in our culture. Instead they are taught to worry about whether the baby is achieving maturational steps on schedule, or preferably ahead of schedule. But however much it might lessen some parents' anxiety, that lock-step approach does not help babies discover themselves.

Anticipating the problems that arise in a child due to external or internal change is essential. For example, the birth of a sibling is a profoundly disturbing event to an older sibling. It makes them wonder, "Am I not enough for my parents?" Their suffering is comparable to what a marital partner would feel if a spouse brought home a new lover.

Murderous emotional thunderstorms are inevitable. Yet this dilemma is normal and not a problem so long as a child is gradually helped to work it out with words and the symbolism of his play. Later in life siblings are generally grateful to have one another.

My first-born granddaughter's play has always been different from her younger sister's. When she was three years old, her favorite game with Grammy (me) was to heap all her dolls in a big pile. Then she and I would pretend we were pregnant by stuffing them up under our shirts, sometimes one at a time, sometimes two, three, or a whole bunch, so that our tee shirts stretched to their limits. We'd wait a while, admiring our swollen bellies, and finally pull the dolls out with happy shouts. "Look! It's a baby girl! And another one! And another!" I had the idea that my granddaughter's game was her way of triumphing over her mother by birthing a big mound of babies instead of just one measly singleton. In the progression of our game, after the new babies were announced and briefly admired, they were tossed aside as if onto a dung heap. Alternatively, we flung them one by one onto the top bunk of her bed before starting over. She was expressing many things with her play, as children do. Her competitiveness with her mother was to be expected, given that she was three, the first Oedipal stage. Her callous mistreatment of her dolls after they had been "born" helped her master her trauma at having a new rival. We played the pregnancy game at least fifty times before her enthusiasm for it began to wane.

Now that my younger granddaughter is three years old, she too plays with dolls, but in a different way from her sister. She carries around "baby," a small fabric doll with a plastic head and extremities. Sometimes she tenderly pats it as it rests on her shoulder; sometimes she dangles it by one limb. She gets anxious when she can't find "baby."

She has the same maternal instinct and rivalry with her mother as her sister had, typical of three-year-old girls, but without as much conflict and anger. She may never suffer the trauma of having a new sibling brought home the way her sister did. She also carries around two other dolls, Mr. and Mrs. Potato Head, which she addresses as Grammy and Grampy. I am flattered, even as I am forced to recognize that our aging heads now resemble potatoes. I also find it hilarious.

In infancy, our relationships with our mother, father, and other family members have a major influence on our developing sense of who we are. First-born children have a slight edge over later-born children in terms of standard I. Q. test scores, middle-born children have an edge in being social, and last-born children an edge in being creative and carefree. Yet, so what? The important thing is to help them all be themselves, with their unique genetic and sibling order givens.

The case of a patient who was *not* raised to be himself comes to mind. He was raised above all to be dutiful, and most of his energy was absorbed in surviving his father's tyrannical needs. As a boy he had to work on the house and yard each weekend without fail, and his father never expressed satisfaction. In a harsh, critical voice, he barked an endless stream of orders at him. His home reverberated with his father's threatening, ridiculing, and belittling tone of voice. His father also smacked him around at the least provocation, as his mother remained passively in the background trying to keep the peace. At family events, the boy was instructed, "Be nice to the relatives." The relatives, in turn, were only interested in whether he had been "a good boy." "How are your grades?" they would ask on meeting him on some holiday occasion. They felt free to criticize him, too: "Can't you see Aunt Ruth's having trouble walking up those steps? Go over and help her already!" He was made to feel guilty for not having had that adult thought on his own.

Fast forward to this boy as a man suffering from obsessive-compulsive disorder. In treatment with me he has become aware that he has spent his life being his parents' "good boy" and hating every minute of it. He has a deep fear of being selfish, but no other internal guideline. He did not want to model himself on his brutal father or his weak and frightened mother. Talking about these things, he has become aware of how resentful he is at having had this "good boy" role foisted upon him. When he wakes up with a migraine, he realizes it is his rage that has been splitting his head open. We both understand that he is without spouse or friends because any time he is with someone, he falls into his old role, automatically putting the other's needs before his own and then feeling enormous resentment. His bitterness is vast. Yet as he talks more and more about it, he is beginning to say "no!" to the parental ghosts. It is terribly hard to face down the echoes of his father's scathing criticisms in the back of his mind, but talking has enabled him to cut his need for medication down to almost zero. He has also brought his new potential for saying "no" into his relationship with me. Instead of being my "good, considerate" patient, he is becoming demanding.

"How are you helping me?" he challenges. "What have you done for me lately?" As he confronts me, I can see the iron rod in his spine relaxing, and the worried scowl on his face dissolving a bit. I am not interested in helping him or anyone else be "good." I am interested in his becoming himself, which means thinking of himself first. I am interested in his becoming self-serving in the sense that the ancient sage Hillel recommended in 30 BC: "If I am not self reliant, on whom shall I rely?" Hillel ends his quote, "If I am selfish, who am I? If not now, when?," but he puts the self resoundingly first, as our mental health requires.

B. IMPRISONED IN FAMILY ROLES

Might an emotionally aware family avoid creating psychic prisons for its children? Is it possible for a family to create a sort of emotional Utopia? If so, how? What might it be like?

When I do family therapy, I use the techniques I have learned for running a therapy group. The goal of group psychotherapy is, "Say everything and help one another to say everything." It is in the process of "saying everything" to one another that we become aware of how different we are from the others around us. Talking enables us to discover the right answers for ourselves and give up our old habits of acquiescing to rules foisted on us long ago. Talking together arouses our respect for others' needs to be the way they are, for if they can be free, so can we.

Jim and June are a high-achieving, middle-aged couple. Though they have weathered many life storms together, they are still prone to creating mutual misery by playing out their old childhood roles. Both had been the responsible oldest siblings in their families, successfully raising their younger siblings in the virtual absence of their alcoholic parents. But shouldering this burden was done at the expense of their own personal development. They learned how to take care of others, but not how to address their own needs. As in any marriage, they imposed their private misery on one another, which is what brought them into my office.

After some months of discussion, I began to notice how Jim went ballistic any time he had the idea that June was trying to make him feel guilty. For example, June reported having said, "I'm hungry. Would it be all right if I order in Chinese food now?" Jim had responded, "I'm not hungry yet." June had taken this as a command and dutifully waited, ignoring her own hunger. Later, when their son told her he was hungry, she had passed the information on to her husband in a tone that implied, "See, you bastard? I'm not the only one around here who is hungry!" Jim had immediately gone to the moon with rage. In place of her actual words, he'd heard an emotional condemnation: "You should have encouraged me to order the food in the first place." After Jim flew off the handle at June, she had withdrawn, and both had wound up in their same old miserable corners.

I see my task as helping each of them become more self-interested: "June! What would it be like if you let your inner bitch come out? You could order food whenever you want, and to hell with whether Jim is hungry or not. He can always reheat his food when he is ready." June looked worried but intrigued. "Would that work?" she asked Jim warily, fully expecting him to scream, "Can't you ever think of what others might need for once in your life?" as her inebriated mother would have done.

"Wow! I'd *love* it!" Jim really wants to see her step forward and be proactive for herself. It will help him do the same for himself. Their session ends with their both thinking of what a pleasure it is to be selfish. They won't have to sacrifice. The other would be an adult perfectly capable of satisfying his/her own needs.

But Jim and June are a repair job. What about something more proactive? I think of Esther, the young mother who worked as a therapist before starting her family. Lately she has been using me as a family coach. Esther has been unhappy with her husband, Rob, because he rarely helps her with the relentless task of raising their two toddlers. He finds every excuse to go out and leave her home alone with them. When he does babysit, he yells at the little ones rather than diverting them from trouble. In addition, Esther has become the chief hostess for their two extended families, preparing frequent feasts for the whole mob. Rob clearly loves playing Lord Bountiful, but he does not help with the preparation or serving of food unless she corners him and insists.

Esther and I discuss his family in our attempt to understand him. Ever since her honeymoon, when her in-laws accompanied them on a trip to Bermuda, Esther has known what a selfish man her father-in-law is. He always grabbed the best seat in the touring car, in the restaurant, in the hotel, and in the theater. He had to be the first one served, the one who hogged the guide's ear, the one who got on and off the bus first, etcetera, ad nauseam. He also treated his wife like a slave, which may have helped drive her into an early grave three years later.

Okay, so there is that appalling influence on her husband. Men want to be like their fathers. Her father-in-law would sooner be caught dead than lift a finger to help manage little kids or do kitchen tasks. But regardless of his love for his father, Rob also loves Esther. The question is, can she influence him without becoming a nag? She and I both know that nagging causes deafness. Her criticizing him in the past had gone nowhere. The most urgent problem is his behavior with the babies, so we tackle that. What will motivate him to learn some new behaviors? Since he wants to please her, there is hope.

"Telling him what to do won't work," I remind her. "Instead you might consult him: 'Should I help you learn how to have fun with your sons?'" After getting his agreement, she could suggest some of the games and songs she uses with them. She could suggest that he "catch them doing something good," instead of responding only when they are "bad." She could also get him thinking about some of the things I have taught her. Best done in a consultative way, she could ask, "You know, toddlers over the age of two get totally defiant when they are bossed around. Instead of, 'You have to go to bed now!,' try just announcing: 'Bedtime!'" Esther could demonstrate by interacting with her boys in front of him. Also, if one of them stubbornly resisted doing something, she could show how she pulls out her trump card by asking, "Will you do this as a favor for me?" Ever eager to please her, they fall into line most of the time. So long as little two- and three-year-olds do not hear a command, they are most likely to cooperate.

Esther could also show her husband how being playful with the little ones gets them to be cooperative. She might say, "Make it sound like a game. Tell the kids, 'Ooh, now we can go put on pajamas, and then I have a really, really silly story to tell you. Who's going to be the first one upstairs?'" Keeping in mind that that was not his father's style of parenting (his style was to walk out of the room and leave everything to his wife), Esther can also be playful with Rob—catch *him* doing something good.

Esther also brings up her problem with her mother, who never seems to want to give her oldest daughter the time of day. Every time she invites her over for a meal, or asks her to watch the babies for a couple of hours, her mother has a reason why she cannot do it. Actually, it is always the same reason—she has to clean her house. When she does agree to come help out, it is with such reluctance in her voice that Esther's guilt ruins her getting a break. She and I study her mother for a bit—another person acculturated to self-sacrifice, always putting her husband's and her own mother's needs before her own. The only people she can say "no" to comfortably are her grown children. Esther decides to give her mother some understanding: "Mom, I never want you to sacrifice yourself for me. You have done too much of that in your life. Please take care of yourself first." Then we'll study whether this relaxes her mother and enables her to have more fun with her daughter and her grandchildren.

Esther often consults me about her three-year-old, a high-energy child who loves to get into everything, touch everything, and defy her when she gives him a command. She has been in the habit of threatening him, but I reflectively question whether that leads to a lot of bad feelings between them, and she acknowledges that this is so. I suggest she work instead with his negative suggestibility. For example, she could tell him to go ahead and do what she does not want him to do, and see what happens. Esther tried it: "I want to stay here," the little boy announced, after Esther told him it was time to leave a store. "Okay," Esther replied. "You can stay here. I'll see you later."

"No, I'll come with you," he immediately reconsidered.

"I want to jump off the diving board," he declared as he climbed up onto it, knowing full well this was off-limits.

"Okay, go ahead" Esther replied.

"No. I changed my mind," the boy said, climbing back down. Esther has learned that whenever she says "No!" or "Don't!" he will defy her. It is a compulsion he shares with most other toddlers. But when she says, "Go ahead!," his anxiety kicks in and he practices being cautious, at least sometimes.

In telling these little anecdotes, I am thinking about how to use healthy emotional education in a family. I come up with my same old admonition: Refrain from using harsh discipline methods. No scolding, no shaming, and no corporal cruelty. Limit giving commands. Instead, work with the children's innate motivation to cooperate—their desire to please mother. Work with their negative suggestibility. The point is to stop and think of a way to turn any encounter into a win/win situation if possible. Kids want to have fun. Husbands want to have fun. Even mothers want to have fun, once their resentments have been acknowledged. Esther has to enlighten her family through gentle understanding and guidance. But she will only have the energy to do this so long as she is good to herself.

Esther is learning to be the chief executive of herself. She has learned that her husband's father is a big baby who can give them almost nothing. She has to let herself know this, so she won't be hurt. Her husband and his siblings are in many ways like their father. Esther does not want to be like her husband's mother was—someone who would sacrifice herself for the men. She was a saint, but then she died of cancer at the age of fifty. She could not say the word "no" to her husband. She could not assert her own needs. Since her cancer was not discovered until it was beyond Stage Four, she had truly neglected herself. One tragedy of Esther's mother-in-law's death was the worry about who would take care of the father. It turns out he can take pretty good care of himself. Just don't ask him for anything. He cannot give. To live in reality is to acknowledge the limitations of others.

Nature's design is for us to become ourselves—inimitable and one of a kind. Evolution, which has given us such rich gifts, cares mainly about preserving our genetic material for the next generation, and the next. Clearly, there is benefit for the heritage of our species in our co-operating with one another to make the world an appropriate environment for our offspring. Yet our technology has outdistanced our limited ability to learn from our experience. We are genetically engineered for the short, brutal lives our ancestors had to endure, and thus to opt for immediate gratification over consideration for the needs of other people or for the environment. A quick result, with a blind eye to the consequences to others, is the default position in human motivation.

I notice how common it is for problem-solving techniques to be self-defeating. For example, people often use teasing or irony or sarcasm to try to persuade others, or rather to shove them, towards change, even though it can plainly be seen that the outcome is the opposite of what they want. Rather than solve a problem, the use of coercion creates further problems. Unconsciously it is a vengeful impulse, based on the wish to punish others when they don't hear us or see things our way. The dilemma is that the infant in any of us can so readily take over: *"I! Me! Mine! Now!"* Our grandiosity in thinking we alone know the right way to think or move forward, our impatience that the other cannot be sensible the way we are, our paranoia invoking our distrust of anyone who comes up with a different decision from ours—these and other impulses blind us to the what is obvious: Money, beauty, possessions, power, are not what make us happy. Our infantile desires goad us to struggle to get them, but once we have them they stale and we look around for what is next. Satisfaction, a feeling of enjoyment in being oneself, is achieved when we are able to understand ourselves and be comfortable with ourselves just as we are and as we are becoming. It is the result of the hard work we invest in getting to know (rather than avoid knowing) ourselves, and then going out and doing whatever is necessary to continue becoming ourselves. On the deepest level, we will discover that some of our desires are destructive, the way a children like to destroy the sand castle they have just sculpted. But given our fundamental ambivalence we will equally discover that some of our desires are constructive, if our lives have not turned us away from others out of bitterness or despair. On balance, it is the loving impulses in our relationships that stir us to create, not destroy, and to enjoy our brief span of years on this planet.

Then what are we to do with all our difficult feelings? Talk. Sit with them. Keep an optimistic attitude. Say friendly things to ourselves. Gregory, an émigré from a Latin American country, spoke about a realization he had on visiting his family back home. "There, everybody is always evaluating other people, making comments about their faults. When my mother picked me up at the airport, she began right away. 'Your brother's wife is doing this and that. . . Who does she think she is? I don't know what is the matter with her.' In this country we look inside at ourselves. We know it is hard enough to solve our own problems. We really can't solve other peoples' problems." Gregory wants to expand beyond his mother's way of comforting herself through seeing others as foolish.

CHAPTER 13

CHOOSING
NOT TO BE
DESTRUCTIVE

A. LEG PAINS

I HAVE TREATED A number of people with addictions, and to a degree I count myself among them. But I will start here by talking about a patient, Mrs. G., for whom developing an addiction has actually been a sign of growth. Two years ago. when I first began meeting with Mrs. G., she only got out of bed to come to her appointments. Her complaint was chronic exhaustion and continuous pains in her legs. On consultation with a psychiatrist, she was given a prescription for anti-depressants and a recommendation for shock therapy.

In her sessions she wept almost constantly but, in time, managed at my suggestion to keep talking through her tears. At first I thought her sadness had to do with her grieving the loss of her first child. However, two years went by and Mrs. G. still could barely muster the strength to get out of bed and care for her second child, who was now six. Mrs. G., an immigrant from an Eastern Europe, lives far away from her mother and other family members. Though she longs for contact with her mother, she has never been able to win her interest and respect. For example, her mother will sometimes accept money from Mrs. G., but any other gift, such as a plant, some new linens, or the offer to buy her a new appliance, is flatly refused or, if given, left unnoticed and unused. Mrs. G.'s sister, too, keeps herself aloof and unavailable. During Mrs. G's visits back home, her sister is always too busy to spend a moment with her. Busy doing what? Washing and ironing, something their mother did compulsively when they were girls. Mrs. G. comes home from these visits in despair, blaming herself for failing yet again to achieve some closeness with them, some recognition from them of her as a sentient being.

Early on in her work with me, Mrs. G. reported elaborate dreams of fixing up her mother's home and property. Many months later, however, she began to dream of calamities befalling the house—walls falling down, water pouring out of a sewer onto the property, and the like. Mrs. G.'s anger was at last making an appearance, with my full encouragement. Becoming able to feel anger is the first step in reversing a depression.

Mrs. G. began to speak with increasing directness about how she felt exploited and misused by her husband's relatives. They would visit her and want to be taken on expensive shopping sprees, always on Mrs. G's credit card. One relative sent over her adolescent daughter—supposedly to get an American college education, except it became clear that the daughter had been misbehaving at home and of course resumed doing so while living with Mrs. G. Yet another relative came to visit because of a medical problem, and Mrs. G. spent a year nursing her and chauffeuring her to many visits to hospitals and doctors. Mrs. G. fulfilled these and other demands selflessly, an angel from heaven, until she began to get the impression that these relatives believed her services and gifts were their entitlement, and that she had become their lackey and a fool.

Finally, she had had enough. She and I came to agree that this lifestyle of being constantly available to others was what her leg pains and extreme exhaustion were about. And then, rather abruptly, her symptom picture changed. Instead of being bedridden with exhaustion and pain, she became an energetic gambler, throwing away considerable amounts of money in a gambling parlor near her home—a case of an instant-onset addiction. What had happened? Like any mental event, it was overdetermined. First, this was Mrs. G.'s initial foray into being a bad girl. For the first time in her life she had cut loose, and what could be more delicious—and overdue? From being passive, obedient, and selfless, she had matured to something like adolescence, which she had never been able to enjoy as a child. Additionally, the guilt, self-defeat, and pain she felt when she lost a pile of money replicated her original emotional home base. Her reward rate from gambling is as frustratingly low as had been her reward rate of getting attention from her mother. It is this second dynamic, I believe, that is the real hook for her, as well as for other addicts I have known. A gambler seeks loss and shame because these feelings repeat their emotional origins in their relationship with their mother. The momentary euphoria from a win (or a drug hit) almost immediately fades as the humiliation and frustration brought on by many losses floods in.

Paradoxically, there is some pleasure in self-defeat—the mostly unconscious feeling of triumph over one's parents (and their symbols) by vanquishing them as they reside in an internal part of the self. Additionally, instead of being the passive victim, now the addict is the one inflicting the pain. Combined, these dynamics constitute the Holy Grail, the true object, of an addict's pleasure in self-destruction.

Could there really be satisfaction be in humiliation, shame, failure, and wasting one's life? The answer, if one is familiar with emotional motivation, is a definite "yes." I have learned never to underestimate the seductive pull of masochism. My hypothesis is that, by repeating the original traumatized feeling experienced with mother, the addict is trying to master it. Instead of achieving this, however, they become ever more dependent on the behavior, on its brief highs and deep lows, as if the addiction is now the yearned for but unavailable mother.

Mrs. G., meanwhile, is becoming more vibrant and alive as she continues to revolutionize her thinking. Instead of being everyone's angel, she is experimenting with other behaviors. Though her husband is dismayed at her gambling, he also finds her new unpredictability exciting. She now has energy to make herself beautiful, and to help her daughter engage with school and life.

In her culture of origin, a wife must be an obedient and dutiful servant to her family. Mrs. G. wanted to be a good wife, but she also had intense, guilt-ridden desires to become something more independent, a person of significance in her own right. She began to speak about her anger to her husband, who was rigidly focused on her fulfilling her "responsibilities." I roped Mr. G. in by asking what his goal was with his wife. When he said, "I want her to be happy," I knew I had him.

I asked, "Should I tell you how to make her happy?" He agreed, but still I double-checked: "If I tell you what to do, will you do it?"

"Yes," he said.

So I told him the two magic words to make her happy: "Yes, dear."

"Okay. I'll do that," he said.

Mrs. G. couldn't believe her ears. She tested him on it: "Will you say 'Yes, dear,' to me even around your relatives?"

"Yes, dear," he said, and they both laughed. They had the best vacation back home of their lives.

B. THE SHORT AND LONG OF IT

Throughout this book I have emphasized the importance of calming down before making a decision about a plan of action. Our emotions make fools of us when we fail to do this. The voice of reason is upstairs in our neocortex, and our emotions are downstairs in our reptilian brain: It is as black and white as that. The choice is whether to be thoughtful and goal oriented, or impulsively give in to our inner snake.

One couple recently came in for marriage counseling. Both were well-educated, accomplished adults over the age of forty, but both had a lifelong habit of letting their feelings rule over their behavior. Major decisions were made in states of anger and resentment. When I asked what their goals were in coming to see me, each immediately began to complain about how the other partner had done this or that in the past. I kept feeling that they expected me to be the lead blanket on their pile of detonating dynamite. I would try to return to my question: "Yes, but the past is gone. What is it that you want me to help you accomplish now and for the future?" I could not get them to say what to me seemed to be obvious: that they wanted to improve their relationship. But in point of fact, they were only interested in indicting one another. In that case, they needed a lawyer, not me.

Perhaps in the past we as a species relied on religion to civilize us: "Do unto others as you would have them do unto you." I agree that this is a sensible guideline, but I welcome the growing scientific evidence that supports it. Studies of the brain show that everything good in civilization comes from using our whole brain—our compassionate prefrontal neocortex, our problem-solving left hemispheric neocortex, our creative, intuitive right hemispheric neocortex, as well as the energy font of the emotional centers in our midbrain. Something in me wants to believe that science and knowledge can be effective. If we learn that the best way to do something is backed by well-researched evidence, then we will choose that way. So here it is: There is a clear and present danger in living "by the seat of the pants" of our emotions, which are mired in a great deal of destructive energy. This is my concern and my caution.

CHAPTER 14

GETTING
IT RIGHT

A. It's All Nursery School

MY COLLEAGUES AND I put on a lot of conferences, seeking to attract people to the training opportunities we offer. Currently, we are planning a conference for teachers. In our brainstorming session, we considered whether we should set up distinct workshops for teachers depending on what grade level they teach. Ultimately we decided to separate those who work in primary schools from those who work in secondary schools. But the thought that kept popping up in my head was, It's all nursery school! because that was when we learned the ABCs of how to deal with our feelings.

I think of the story my patient Esther told me about her three-year-old son's recent birthday party. As was her custom, she had invited members from her husband's family as well as members from her own. And, as usual, the two families exhibited great distrust of one another: They visibly did not "get along." Instead, representatives from each side told Esther their criticisms of the other side. Esther's family thought her in-laws were too standoffish; her in-laws complained that those on her side were talkative and shallow. One of her husband's cousins went right up to Esther's grandmother, who habitually clutches her purse to her bosom like a shield, and emphatically suggested, "Why don't you just put your pocketbook down?" The comment was well intended, but Grandmother was outraged. Her pocketbook is her security blanket!

Then a cousin from Esther's side asked, "Why is your husband's family so shy?"

Esther couldn't understand why they couldn't all just relax and enjoy themselves. Why were they so uncomfortable? They acted if they felt threatened! Were they competing for her loyalty? How come they couldn't simply focus on the cute little three-year-olds enjoying new toys for a couple of hours, to say nothing of the delicious food she provided? How come they couldn't act like grown-ups for her?

My reaction to Esther was to take fault with my field. How come we therapists haven't taught everyone to expect that a social occasion mixing strangers together will arouse a lot of anxiety? How come we haven't taught people how to help one another through the unavoidable awkwardness we feel when we are making new acquaintances? How come we haven't helped everyone be comfortable with the fact that, whenever we are in a new setting, we regress to the way we felt in nursery school—scared, tense, lonely, and wanting our mommy? How come we haven't helped people bridge the gulf of strangeness and reach toward the opportunity of enjoying someone new? After all, this is reality. All these feelings are real, ordinary, and quite uncomfortable. When faced with frustration, the question is how to make the best of a difficult moment, but somehow we therapists have yet to make this common knowledge.

What I have tried to teach in this book is an extension of what we learned in kindergarten before crossing the street. "Stop, look, and listen before stepping off the curb." In that pause, our cerebral cortex can align with our emotions to figure out the most sensible course of action. In a social setting, some part of our empathetic prefrontal cortex will remind us that everyone else is most likely feeling anxious, too. Meanwhile, our playful right brain might think of some amusing way to bridge the gap. Together these and other brilliant parts of our mind can come up with novel tactics. If the two sides of Esther's family could get to know one another, they would find out they have things in common. There is the weather, the season, the local ball teams, the economic crisis, to comment about in the search for common ground. Yes, it is hard. Those old, miserable nursery school feelings of being alone and abandoned intrude. But our cortical brain knows those reluctances and fears are just. . .feelings. Our cortical brain knows things will go best if we have empathy for one another. It can find ways to lessen the wariness that interferes with our getting to know the miracle that each stranger truly is, despite any incompatibilities.

This is emotional education, in my view. Give yourself permission to have all your feelings, and then mentally climb up into your cortex and create ways to be civilized. Ask one easy and friendly question of the stranger at the gathering. Do an "intake." Here are the questions I ask in an initial interview with a patient:

"What brought you here today?"

"Tell me the story of your life. You can begin anywhere."

In a social situation I extrapolate:

"What brought you here today?"

"Are you on the groom's side or the bride's side?"

"Have you tried the hostess's eggplant paté?"

"Are you a movie fan? Have you seen that new film about spiders?"

Sooner or later I hit the right note, and the conversation begins to flow. Making friends is hard at first but worth it once we find that something which connects us. We did it in nursery school in side-by-side play, and now we can use words. Cautiously we sidle past our distrust and begin to have fun. We're a social species. It is how we thrive.

B. Becoming Myself

My mother once asked why my sister and I married the men we did, men who, from her point of view, were totally unsuitable. After giving it some thought, my sister replied, "Because they let us be who we are." It's true. Though, when we were young, we could not have articulated it, my sister and I shared an ideal of wanting to become ourselves, not passively take on my mother's way of life. For my mother's generation, this was an alien thought. She believed our main task in adulthood was to find a man with some power and wealth, and keep house for him the way she had done, as had her mother before her. Her belief system required obedience to the societal norms of the 1940s and 1950s. She could not conceive that that idea was abhorrent to us.

"You've got to conform!" she once shrieked after finding out that my sister, aged sixteen, had a date with someone outside of our ethnic group. "God damn it! You must!" My mother was in a state of panic, as if her life depended upon our neighbors not "thinking less" of her. The generation gap between her and the two of us came to seem as wide and uncrossable as the Mississippi River in full spring flood. What was important to her didn't compute for the two of us. We wanted something different from the gift of life.

The goal of psychotherapy is to become oneself. By telling the story of our lives, we have a chance to examine all the old influences that continue to affect us. We have a chance to sort out the ones that are mainly undigested emotional reactions from those that involve the higher, gentler, civilized, neocortical parts of our brain. It gives us the opportunity to choose which ones we want to retain, and which to lessen or discard. Unless we talk and think about them, they lurk in the background, ready to bully us into a submissive mood or an action whenever our guard is down. That is the nature of our mind with its compelling memories and patterns.

If I were a politician, I would support a platform based on reflective, cooperative talk among all the candidates. I would promote the honest and humble expression of feelings. I would sort out the candidates who are driven by power or greed from those who want the greatest good for the country and the world. If necessary, I might request the use of an FMRI—functional magnetic resonance imaging—to check whether their thinking indicated well-integrated higher cortical decision making versus primitive emotional impulsivity. Shouts, insults, threats, shaming, and ridiculing would be eliminated from my ideal political discourse. Sly innuendoes meant to incite rage or humiliation would be debunked. The goal would be to promote the common weal in an atmosphere of honesty and respect. The voice of reason is soft, whereas the voice of emotions is loud and self-serving. It is a primitive part of our brain that delights in skirmishing with and humiliating others. Cassandra-like, I dream about a better world.

Becoming myself through psychotherapy is a gift that has freed me to please myself. This is in stark contrast to the repeated admonitions I received as a little girl: "Don't be selfish! Always think of others first." After a while I figured out that, although grown-ups said things like this, they didn't actually practice them. I developed a good nose for hypocrisy. Anyway, now that I see that it is very difficult to figure out how to please myself, I realize it is all but impossible to please anyone else unless we discuss things and negotiate for quite a while.

Pleasing myself means trying to figure out what is right for me, moment by moment. No one else on this planet knows the answer, not even my husband of forty-plus years. I engage in fantasy research: What would it be like to do this or that, choose this or that, be this or that? What would it be like if I mother myself, soothe myself, admire myself, agree or disagree with myself, indulge or deprive myself? Often I have no answer, or a multiplicity of answers, so I do nothing. I have learned I have to work at being a constructive companion to myself, a job no one else can fulfill, at least not beyond a narrow limit, and not for long, though I welcome all attempts.

Pleasing myself also involves granting myself the right to reject what I don't want. Don't give me a guilt trip, for I will ridicule it, at least in my head. Until someone has walked miles in my shoes, how can he know what is true or meaningful about or for me? Don't poke your voice with an edge on it as a weapon into my ears. I'll mentally reject that, too. Here's what I silently say, a lot of which I learned from my inner-city teenagers:

"You ain't all that either," or

"Your mother wears combat boots." (I have no idea why that got them so incensed, but it truly did, so it is indelibly and deliciously etched in my mind.) Some other come-backs I learned from a comedian friend: "You don't like what I said? So sue me! Go call a cop!" And, "Yeah, you couldn't find your ass in a telephone booth, both hands free!" Old retorts from when I was in kindergarten come in handy, too: "I'm rubber, you're glue. Everything you say to me bounces off of me and sticks to you." And "Sticks and stones will break my bones, but names will never harm me." I don't have to say these things out loud. Silently, to myself, is enough.

Uninvited advice is out the door: "Big whoop!" I inwardly hoot at a friend who always suggests improvements to any thought or decision I express. My silent response: "What makes you think I didn't have that thought already, you jerk?"

Telemarketers, get ready to hear the latest click! TV commercials, click! Style mongers, sayonara. Now, what a joy—a gift!—to explore my very own feelings, guilt-free! The full combustion of my emotions! Exuberance!

I reflect upon the last time my husband asked what I wanted for my birthday. "I'd really like a gold bracelet. I saw a terrific one in Costco the other day." He came home with a bangle, when what I had wanted was a chain. How could he not have known what I had so clearly pictured in my mind? Once again, there it was—the same old disappointment. Why did I have to spell it out for him? Only, now my secondary reaction is to reflect,

"(Giggling): How come he can't hear the words I haven't said?" We are still working on getting our communication right. Now that we are both resigned to the fact that we are each full of such folly, it can be so funny. We laugh and laugh.

I hear outrage from others about the disappointing gifts they receive. A college student and her mother rush to the store, where her fiancé bought her an engagement ring, to see how much he paid. Okay, that has some sort of meaning for them, yet I can't but wonder if he knows what he is in for. Were they suspicious about his generosity? Did they have doubts about his ability to be a provider? Why was her mother intruding on her daughter's love life?

My patient Tom is deeply hurt that his girlfriend's birthday gift for him cost so little. Not only was it under a hundred dollars, it was wrong in other ways, as if she had not known what was in his heart. After all, he had been so munificent with her.

"Did you tell her what you would like?" I asked.

"Well, no, but if she loved me wouldn't she have known?" Ah. He wants her to read his mind. Well, that won't happen on *this* planet! I explore:

"Has anyone ever given you a perfect present?"

"No."

"Have you ever gotten one for your self?"

"Of course!" He lists several. We stumble upon the fact that we are the only experts when it comes to getting ourselves perfect gifts.

I give myself stuff constantly. A delicious sandwich, a new suit, toys for my grandkids. I award myself totally comfortable shoes, permission never to weigh myself, and to be fussily vegetarian most of the time. I authorize myself not to cook, not to worry, not to read horrible news beyond the headlines, unless I want to. I lavish myself with time wasted browsing through catalogs, musing about things I might buy—the gift of daydreams. I bestow forgiveness on myself for making expensive mistakes, for throwing things away, for getting a parking ticket.

Though I take it for granted, almost like the air I breathe, my psychotherapy is what has enabled me to meet Freud's hallmark of emotional well-being—"able to love and to work." Far from the fearful gloom of my youth, my thoughts have become predominantly—-though not exclusively—breezy. Having become tolerant of myself has made me tolerant of others, as well as philosophical about the inevitable tragedies we all face. My mind has been freed to roam where it will, and wherever it goes I can trust it to serve me in some way. Of course I can still fall into a mood of anxiety or despair. I would not have it otherwise. I am my feelings, all of them—I could not lose one without losing them all. But my recovery time from the darkest ones is so much briefer than in my youth.

In my head, my thoughts, memories, whims—often in half formed bits and pieces—flow, pivot, disintegrate, reform, go here, and go there. Some are wishful, some are purposeful, some are annoyances, and some are guilt ridden. Some are cruel and destructive, but no less human for all that. I am pleased to be aware of them, lest I inadvertently act on them. I float comfortably from curiosity to pride to anxiety to love to hate to a task on my "to do" list. My thoughts dissolve into one another like movie scenes. Ideas flash in, solutions to problems I hadn't been aware I was addressing.

I am sometimes taken aback by having my first thought on awakening be of terminal illness, either my own or that of someone dear to me. I realize my sleeping mind has been working on this scariest aspect of my current reality. One recent nightmare was a vision of myself as a shapeless, bent, crone standing alone on a sidewalk. I studied my thoughts: *Hmm, am I rehashing my old worries about being unlovable in this current guise?* My next thought was a backwash of reassuring calmness: *Ah well, been there before. . . .* Then up cropped an association: Jeff, a patient in his fifties, had told me an anecdote the day before of how he had been a Good Samaritan to an elderly woman who had fallen on the sidewalk, smashing her teeth through her lip. He had helped her get up and then accompanied her by cab to a nearby hospital, where the doctor called him a saint. So there it was—"Monkey see, monkey do." The childish wish in my dream was to get similar treatment from this kind and handsome man. Weeks later I had a similar dream, only this time I was my current age, and the one who helped me up was a woman. Again, a patient's anecdote of being helped up by a woman friend after a fall came to mind. But who was the woman in my dream? Was it my mother? Will I go on wishing for her all my life? Probably. Oh, well.

My waking mind recoups.

Each of my patients is a gift, just as each of my high school students once was, my current students still are, and my family members and colleagues and associates always will be. Having studied hundreds of people through the years, I confirm and reconfirm what I know about the mind, my own and others', even as I learn or relearn new things. Healing others I keep on healing myself. People seek my services because they are suffering in some way. I suffer, too. I find that our distress results mainly from a habit of criticizing ourselves, an act most of us were raised to view as virtuous. Of course we also suffer from memories that we need to grieve, from fears based on misinformation about the nature of the mind, from longings based on unmet needs for nurturance, and from just plain reality. Slowly, I open my patients to new ways of thinking and feeling about themselves. In the process I retrain myself, and on it goes.

At a recent professional meeting, I looked around at the familiar faces of my friends as they entered the room. Hugging one, I reminded her of our joint connection to a dear colleague who had died two years previously. Our painful sighs commingled. Greeting another, I recalled her telling me how, back home in the Dominican Republic, everybody—without exception!—danced at any social gathering. I drifted into a reverie about what it would be like to dance with everyone there in the meeting room. What would it be like to move together in joyous tempos, back-to-back and belly-to-belly? To Texas two-step, boogie, jig, folk dance, square dance, bop, and twist? How about let's tango, waltz, mambo, samba, salsa, and swing our booties? Let's take a break from all this thinking! *Bailamos!* Let's dance into the sunset, into the moon, and into life and dreams and hope! Life is so short. Let's dance together now and always!

REFERENCES

Bettelheim, B. (1976). *The uses of enchantment.* New York: Random House.

Bronte, C. (2008). *Jane Eyre.* New York: Signet Classic. [First published 1844].

Eckstein, R. (1969). *From learning for love to love for learning.* New York: Brunner Mazel.

Erikson, E. H. (1950). *Childhood and society.* New York: Norton.

Goleman, D. (1995). *Emotional intelligence.* New York: Bantam Books.

Kandel, E. (2006). *In search of memory,* New York: W.W. Norton.

LeDoux, J. (1998). *The emotional brain: The mysterious underpinnings of emotional life.* New York: Simon & Schuster.

LeDoux, J. (2002). *Synaptic self.* New York: Viking.

Panksepp, J. (1998). *Affective neuroscience: The foundations of human and animal emotions.* London: Oxford University Press.

Pepys, S. (1925). *The diary of Samuel Pepys, 1660–1669.* London: Dent.

Piontelli, A. (2002). *From fetus to child: An observational and psychoanalytic study.* London: Routledge.

Terr, L. (1990). *Too scared to cry.* New York: Harper & Row.

Thomas, L. (1974). *Lives of a cell: Notes of a biology watcher.* New York: Viking.

Saint Exupery, A. (1971). *The little prince.* New York: Harcourt Brace.

Selye, H. (1956). *The stress of life.* New York: McGraw Hill.

Winnicott, D. (1958). Hate in the countertransference. In *Collected papers: Through pediatrics to psycho-analysis.* New York: Basic Books.

This book has been set in Hoefler's *Requiem*,
derived from a set of inscriptional capitals appearing in
Ludovico Vicentino degli Arrighi's 1523 writing
manual, *Il Modo de Temparere le Penne.*